Cool, than for all I am so here 'grateful -- it is! love, James *James Mabely*

Why Follow Rules?
Trust your Intuition

James Maberly

Published by James Maberly
www.cultivating-intuition.com

Why Follow Rules?

Cover design; Victorine Lieske - www.indiebookcovers.blogspot.co.uk

A catalogue record for this book is available from the British Library

ISBN no. 978-0-9575826-2-0

To my family; Veronica, Ted, Harry, Jasper and JoJo.
Thank you for everything. You are amongst my
greatest teachers.

I love you all.

Main donors towards publication costs

Fifty two people very generously contributed towards the cost of
publication for this book. They are all listed on the website and
I am most grateful to all of them for their vision and support.
In particular, I wish to mention two who gave extremely
generously. Scott Russell and Ernie Patterson, thank you both so
much for showing your confidence in this book. I offer you my
very grateful thanks.

*"How easy it is to get covered over by all of the rules and the controls and the perceptions of life.
How easy it is to negotiate yourself away from your enlightenment."*

Adamus St Germain

Preface

Writing this book has been an exciting and fascinating journey. When I started out I felt I already knew what to write. Little did I realise that in the process of writing it I would have learnt so much more about myself, others and the whole subject of rules and intuition. Thank you as the reader for allowing me this privilege. If it were not for you I may never have taken the journey in quite the same way.

I believe we are our own best guides as to when we are ready to learn, even if we are not conscious of it. We learn some pretty good lessons early on from our teachers, parents, elders and books but we only learn the important lessons of life as and when we are ready to do so. Thus I assume that those who read this will do so because they are on a journey of exploration as I was (and still am). I hope you enjoy the experience.

I have several people to thank for their assistance in the writing of this book. I would like to thank my family for their patience and their constructive ideas that have assisted me along the way and for allowing me to use anecdotes about them and some of their art images throughout the book. To Binkie Andrews for her regular assistance with typing, proof reading, friendship and excellent advice; to Keir Wyatt, for his help in proof reading and his wise counsel; to Mandi Rukuni for his friendship, support and advice; to Josee Honeyball for her consistent support; to Alan Doyle for his scrupulous proof reading and questioning mind and for our camaraderie in the self-publishing arena; to Charles Boscawen for his important input; to Sam Passow for his considered and useful guidance; to Monique Drummond for her insight; to Seymour Jacklin for his clear vision and editorial eye; to Victorine Lieske for such a wonderful cover and to Jason Mathews for his continued responses to my many questions.

I have two friends whose work and wisdom have inspired me greatly over the years and have played a very important part in the formulation of this book. The first is Ken Anderson whom I have known for many years and the second is Charles Handy. His 'Thoughts for the day' audio tape remains one of my most treasured possessions. The website (detailed below) has been set up in order for those interested to find further information, links to books, talks and courses that encourage us to think and act differently and to remind us again of the extraordinary facility our intuition offers us in our everyday existence.

James Maberly
Suffolk, United Kingdom
June 2014

Visit **www.cultivating-intuition.com** *for more background, links to talks, images, references and a regular blog of new ideas.*

Table of Contents

1

So what is Intuition?

Intuition is the birth place of all original thought.

Everyone has intuitive thoughts every day, whether we recognise them as such or not. Some are highly original. It was intuition that gave Nikola Tesla[1], the brilliant Serbian-American inventor the source for his extraordinary ideas. It gave Einstein, Leonardo da Vinci, Benjamin Britten and Richard Branson theirs and it also gives the poet who lives next door to us the source of her creative thoughts as well. Steve Jobs of Apple fame has often said he lived by his intuition.

When puzzling out some challenging problem which simply does not seem to add up or to make sense to us, our minds often go round and round in circles. Often the moment we relax and drift away from our incessant thoughts, the necessary information comes through in a sudden burst of clarity and a 'Eureka' moment occurs.

At the moment of arrival of an inspirational idea (let's call it a 'spark'), the mind has not yet kicked in. The 'spark' arrives quietly without fanfare (often at unusual times), deposits itself in our minds and waits for us to decide whether we want it or not. If not, then it simply disappears. If the 'spark' prompts us to apply active thought and work out how to complete our puzzle, then that is our 'Eureka' moment.

Whatever the puzzle or challenge is, the method or approach by which we choose to respond to this unique inspiration is entirely our own because it is coloured by each of our personalities and the multitude of experiences we have had in our lifetimes. By continuing to listen to the original 'sparks' that flash into our minds at each stage of the creative process, what emerges is an original idea which is uniquely ours. Whether we decide to make use of that thought, expand it and effectively 'bring it to life' is also entirely up to us. We are the creators - the choice is ours, or to make it more personal, mine.

I asked myself, 'can you and will you stand up and make your mark or are you too tied to the 'norms' and rules of the society around you? Will you relax into and follow your heart or will you do as so many do and let the ideas slip by, foiled by the need to conform or the fear of losing a steady income to pay the bills'?

In the chapters that follow I provide questions, thoughts and considerations I have encountered along my own journey on how to develop an intuitive idea into something tangible and effective and there is far more to it than one might imagine. Some people are very good at this but there are not nearly enough. We need original thinkers now more than ever. We need them to break away from the stereotypical systems, rules and structures of the past and emerge with new and vibrant ideas for the future. We need more people to step forward and make the necessary changes needed in our society. It requires a shift in our appreciation of ourselves and our abilities and a better understanding of the nature of our inner core, the root of all our creativity, innovation and originality.

Original thought is critical to our future progress. Engage with it, own it and bring it to life. The power to do so is in our hands.

[1] *Nikola Tesla invented fluorescent lighting, the Tesla induction motor, the Tesla coil, the alternating current (AC) electrical supply system that included a motor and transformer, and 3-phase electricity. Tesla is now also credited with inventing modern radio.*

Two Intuitive drawings made using found objects by Xenia Dautzenberg aged 11 (made at extraordinary speed)

2

Intuition: going beyond the mind

Intuition: the ability to understand something instinctively, without the need for conscious reasoning; Knowledge or belief obtained neither by reason nor by perception; instinctive knowledge or belief independent of any reasoning process; the quality or ability of having direct perception or quick insight.
Sources: Oxford, Collins, Merriam-Webster, Dictionary.com, Wikipedia.

Albert Einstein realised the power of his intuition. He recognised that inspiration comes from beyond us and that we have lost sight of its true value. He wrote: *"The Intuitive mind is a sacred gift and the rational mind is a faithful servant. We have created a society that honours the servant and has forgotten the gift."*[1]

As mentioned in Chapter 1, another genius who recognised that inspiration came to him through his intuition was the inspired Serbian-American inventor, Nikola Tesla. Not only did Tesla recognise the power of his intuition, he also had visions that were so clear to him that he could actually see the full workings of his ideas before he had even put thought and reason into the process.

Jonas Salk, the inventor of the polio vaccine wrote that *'The intuitive mind tells the thinking mind where to look next.'*[2]

Both of the above quotations remind us that intuition is the source of all originality. The logical mind takes that spark of intuition and molds it into something more tangible by helping us to expand on ideas we may already have or by cultivating new and original ideas.

They also both suggest that there is such a thing as the 'intuitive mind'. This is what I refer to as the 'intuitive self'; it is entirely separate from the mind as we know it and the idea that we have a 'conscious thought' about one thing and a 'spark of inspiration' about something else suggests immediately that there is a separation between the two. The intuitive self works with the mind but is separate from it, just as the ego is separate from it also.

Consider that the left and right sides of the brain need each other to function correctly. Equally, they both need information to process. Images, thoughts, sounds, smells and all manner of information are entering our brains all the time whilst we go about our daily tasks and the brain processes that information in order to make sense of it all. We discern the feelings and emotions of others around us through sight, sound and touch and through sensing the energy they are radiating outwards. All this we know and we do automatically.

Intuition picks up on the information which we are processing and drops ideas (particles if you like) into our minds on a regular basis and most of the time we ignore them as we are either busy, already engrossed in some task that does not require intuition to further our aims or because we have taken on board the teachings through religion or through education that intuition is unreliable and cannot be trusted. Some religions are consciously counter-intuitive which is a great shame and is perhaps one of the reasons why some of them are stuck so solidly in the past and not shifting with the times into a new, exciting and creative world.

After a fair amount of time considering and indeed listening to my intuitive self, I have come to realise that the mind is not the primary driving force within us. It is important and crucial to our daily existence but in reality the mind is simply a tool to be used constructively. It is a processor which we can use to our advantage and it has the capacity to process information logically and creatively, allowing us to move our societies forward. The primary driving force however is the heart, where the soul resides, and that is part of the intuitive self.

This is a difficult point to argue but can be clearly understood when we consider the music and songs we listen to on a daily basis. How many of them concentrate on subjects such as maths, geography, French, the stock market, engineering, diplomacy or the Royal Bank of Scotland? Do we sing about real estate, driving conditions or traffic cones? Most songs, most musical communications and most poetry relate to love in its many guises; desperate love, lost love, rejection, unrequited love, a need for love or relationships in general. When all is said and done we are driven by the impulses of the heart, not by the mind. If someone is rude to you, you feel hurt. If you win a prize you feel elated. If your girlfriend or boyfriend walks out on you, it seriously messes up your ability to concentrate and be productive at work. If you have a brilliant idea, which has great potential, it is not the reasoning behind it that will make it work. It is the feeling you have about your own ability to make it happen, and where does that come from? The heart.

It is also from exactly this point that the spark of intuition comes and it emerges quietly and beautifully as described in the definition above, without inference or the use of reason and before the mind has kicked in. It simply drops into your mind and allows you to decide what to do with it. Some people block it and take no notice. Others consider it then let it go. Still others, particularly those who are creative and entrepreneurial examine these sparks, choosing which of them catch their imaginations and expand them into constructive and original thoughts.

Are intuition, instinct and 'gut' feelings the same thing?

These are often considered one and the same. There is no hard and fast definition, so each of us must feel comfortable with what we choose to believe ourselves. For some, it is just a mix of words to describe the intuitive impulse.

My experience tells me they are not the same. Intuition has a different source of information, coming to us through our heart space, where our soul resides, directly connected to the infinite intelligence that surrounds us and of which we are a part. It is quiet, pure and, whilst relevant to what we may be doing at the time it arrives, covers an infinite array of different topics. A 'gut' feeling on the other hand is based on learned experience, either good or bad. Thus for example, if you are a very experienced engineer, you can make 'gut' decisions relating to your subject very quickly because of your already 'learned' information. If on the other hand you are new to the job, the gut response may not carry the necessary knowledge to provide the same level of guidance. I would suggest that we often receive 'gut' feelings in the same way as we receive intuitive information and as a result we assume they are one and the same. The results of both working together can of course be extraordinarily valuable.

Instinct is something altogether different. We have certain instinctive responses (as animals do) already programmed into us. For example if someone lunges at me, I will instinctively protect my face. There is no thought process involved whatsoever. Yet some people will say they have an instinctive feeling about something or 'my instinct tells me..'. I believe this is simply a matter of semantics and what it being referred to is an intuitive spark or feeling or indeed a 'gut' or learned response.

Jake Barnett[3], a young man in the USA with an IQ of 189 (higher than Einstein's) who at the age of 14 is studying for a Master's Degree in Quantum Mechanics might be described as a child genius. Diagnosed with Asperger's Syndrome (autism) when two, the 'special needs' community had determined that it was likely that he would never read. Their objectives were to teach him basic life skills, given his condition. His mother decided differently. She says she 'instinctively' knew that this was wrong adding that she would 'follow her instincts' for his future which indeed she has done as his whole learning experience has been very intuitive. I believe that what she is describing is her intuition as it fits perfectly with my understanding of how it works so I would reiterate once more, there is no hard and fast definition, so please feel comfortable with whatever words sound right for you.

Having a 'gift'

When a youngster appears to have a remarkable 'gift' for something be it art, music, science or anything else (like Jacob Barnett), we describe it as 'genius' – it is the only way we can rationalise it. It can't be as a result of 'learned' information (since there is no previous experience) so it must be something else. Some would suggest it is all in the mind, but the mind is merely a processor. It needs the input first, like petrol for a car. So how does this knowledge arrive? How are they so remarkably skilful so quickly?

Perhaps their whole experience is more intuitive than we realise and that they are much more open to this amazing asset that we have at our disposal, allowing themselves easy, constant and direct access to it as they further develop their skills. For some, the intuitive impulse is very strong and allows for a very fast development. One young lady I know seems quite shy much of the time but hand her a pencil or a paintbrush and she transforms into a confident, competent, creative and original young artist. As a participant in one of my Intuitive Drawing courses, the speed with which she produced her images was quite extraordinary and I was almost unable to keep up with her as I moved around with my camera taking photos.

Not to be confused with common sense

Do not confuse intuition with common sense as they are completely different. Common sense is the application of the mind to various 'needs and requirements', using a balance of knowledge and reason. It may well be that intuition assists in the determination of a common sense decision but they remain completely separate concepts.

Where does intuition come from?

We are surrounded by a world made up of the most astounding beauty, balance and symbiosis. Everything has its place and has a role to play in the grand scheme of things. Every leaf has a beautiful constitution and every insect is perfectly designed for its particular role. When the leaf drops off and the insect dies, the remains add to the nutrients required by the soil in order to stimulate the growth of more plants, trees and grasses which are then eaten or used by other creatures in order to survive. There is an extraordinary intelligence in everything. It is as if every cell brings with it its own intelligence and acts upon it as necessary. What we also know is that when the smallest particle of anything at all is broken down in a particle accelerator, it is in fact nothing at all. No 'thing' exists; it is just pure energy.

Everything around us is therefore made up of the same 'stuff' as we are; pure energy. We also know that we are affected by the energy of everything around us all of the time. Perhaps the easiest way to understand it is to think of electrical energy or the heat of the sun. Another is being with someone who is depressed and lonely and feeling your energy being drained out of you.

Through our energy fields, we are connected to this supreme intelligence that exists all around us and that is the source of our intuition. The main religions would refer to this power as God, whilst others have different names like Wakan Tanka[4], which means 'Great Mystery'. And by the way, we are most certainly not the only creatures who can access it. You may recall that when the Tsunami struck in Asia several years ago, animals began moving inland and away from the water long before the Tsunami struck. How did they know to do that? Some would argue that they have an inherent intuitive ability to sense changes in the weather, the atmosphere and the energy all around them and they respond to it. Well exactly!

In his book 'Dogs that know when their owners are coming home', Scientist Rupert Sheldrake documents countless incidents in which animals use their intuition (he refers to it as the sixth sense) to determine their next move and explores ways in which animals can teach us to question the boundaries of conventional scientific thought. He suggests that much that seems paranormal at present looks completely normal when we expand our ideas of normality.

It is intuition which has brought us to where we are and intuition which will inspire us along the route to where we are going. It is a shame that intuition is not given its true value but if you take anything away from this book it is this, so beautifully expressed by Einstein. *"The Intuitive mind is a **sacred gift** and the rational mind is a **faithful servant**. We have created a society that honours the servant and has forgotten the gift."* Let us once more honour the gift and recognise its place in our extraordinary progress and remember that the mind is not the 'be all and end all' – it is a rational servant, a tool to be used wisely and as necessary, to assist us on our way.

"If prayer is you talking to God, then intuition is God talking to you."

Dr Wayne Dyer 'Everyday Wisdom', Hay House Inc.,
Carlsbad, CA, 1993

[1] *2009, 'Einstein on Cosmic Religion and Other Opinions and Aphorisms' by Albert Einstein, Dover Publication, Mineola, New York. (This Dover edition is an unabridged republication of 'Cosmic Religion and Other Opinions and Aphorisms', originally published in 1931 by Covici-Friede, Inc., New York).*

[2] *Jonas Edward Salk (1914 –1995) was an American medical researcher and virologist, best known for his discovery and development of the*

first successful polio vaccine.

[3] Jacob Barnett is an American teenager with an IQ of 189, currently studying for a Masters Degree in Quantum Mechanics at the age of 14. More about him in Chapter 5.

[4] Wakan Tanka is the term for 'the Sacred' or 'the Divine' or 'Great Mystery', as used by the Sioux Indians in America.

3

Creativity; synergy between intuition and the mind

"Too much thought kills creativity whilst intuition brings it to life."

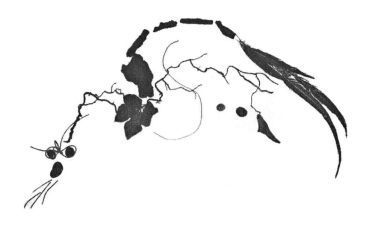

Intuitive drawing with found objects by Christina Orrock

I run an intuitive drawing course from my studio. The purpose of the course is first of all to encourage people, through a series of exercises, to recognise and work with their intuition. Here, using a variety of bits and pieces i.e. leaves, stones, twigs, wire, flowers and many other objects, I encourage participants to place them onto a sheet of paper without prior thought, simply responding to their intuition. People are constantly amazed at how creative they are without even trying. I also encourage them to draw intuitively to the sound of different types of music. Some drawings are huge – some very small, but all characterised by an amazing spontaneity of action.

On completion of these exercises, I encourage participants to go back and look at what they have produced over the previous two days and begin a process of deriving potentially creative ideas from these 'drawings' and see where that leads. This is where the mind begins the process of engaging with the intuitive 'sparks' which have emerged and helps to solidify them into creative ideas. As we engage the mind in this thought process, so our intuition is once more ignited and we will continue to receive more intuitive 'sparks' which we can either respond to or ignore, further developing our creative thoughts and ideas.

Intuitive drawing – responding to different types of music

Once they are ready to do so, I encourage participants to draw or paint another piece (or pieces), which have developed in their mind as a direct response to their previous intuitive drawings.

What emerges from participants are 'drawings' that are new, invigorating and different to what they might normally produce. These emerge the way they do as we focus less on how good at drawing and painting we are and more on allowing the ideas to develop spontaneously; in other words, we change the focus from the 'academic' and 'egoical' to the 'organic' and allow the ideas to flow. It is often extraordinary how quickly some people can work and how inspiring their ideas are once they can 'escape' from the trap of egoical programming.

Considered drawing of a tree drawn to the sound of vibrant music.

Our greatest limitation – the egoical self

The greatest limitation to our creativity and originality is not in our abilities; rather, it stems from our lack of faith and belief in ourselves and consequently in our own competence. It causes us to 'toe the line' rather than to try something different because the very act of stepping out of line challenges our belief in ourselves and the result might well be painful. Thus many of us often take the easy route and either do nothing or something comfortable which is usually predictable. This lack of self-belief generally stems from experiences we have had as children, which become so engrained that they affect us for the rest of our lives. They become part of our egoical perceptions of ourselves.

Once we recognise that creativity and ability are inherent

within us, it helps us realise that we are capable of so much more than we have come to believe. What we begin to see is that if we work more from our intuition, unhindered by the ego, we can be remarkably creative and original.

The World Peace Game - an exercise in developing and recognising intuition, creativity and understanding in children[1]

John Hunter is an inspired teacher from Richmond, Virginia in the USA who developed an extraordinary game in which he encouraged his classes of nine-year-old children to look at global problems that most of us, as adults would consider overwhelming. The game is presented on four levels on a flexi-glass structure with a space level, a sky level, ground level and an underground/underwater level. The scenario involves four countries all with certain assets and each country has a prime minister and a cabinet. There is also a World Bank and the United Nations involved and even more besides. He presents them with a 13-page crisis document with 50 interlocking problems so that as one thing changes, everything else changes.

The success of the game has been remarkable. What John has come to realise is that these children, still largely unaffected by adult limitations of self-worth, income, status and history and of course his own belief in their ability to deal with these issues, are able to come up with the most amazing solutions to these problems. Their assessments and actions are much more intuitive than those of an adult would be (burdened by years of study and structure) and thus their concepts and ideas flow more naturally and have no restrictions. He is constantly amazed at not only their creativity but also the wisdom they both gain and express whilst playing the game, particularly with relation to non-violence, peace and collectively working together for the greater good, all of which they discover for themselves.

A constant process of development

Creativity is the result of intuition and the mind working closely together, fostered by us as the creators. Our history, knowledge and experience, blended with a realisation that we are capable of coming up with thoughts and ideas of real value are the starting points for original thought. It is important to recognise though that the first original idea that comes might not be the final one. It may need some modification along the way and thus may need a fair amount of persistence. Run with it. It is a vital part of the creative journey.

Sometimes what might appear to be a gross error of judgement or alternatively a poorly created object or drawing may actually be the source of an idea or design that takes us several very large paces forward, so it is important not to chastise ourselves for what might appear to be below standard work. I remember once making a drawing that I felt was very weak which after many attempts to adjust, I ripped into tiny pieces, though luckily not before I had taken a photograph. Years later I came across that photo and surprised myself with what I saw – it was inspiring and became the source of some new and exciting work.

There is nothing more invigorating than allowing your creativity the freedom to express itself. If being creative is a challenging concept, then give yourself permission to have a go. If the journey sounds interesting, then through the pages of this book you will find some concepts and ideas that may ignite your own creativity and allow you the freedom to engage yourself in the cultivation of some really original ideas and thoughts.

Intuitive images throughout the book

Throughout the book you will find additional examples of intuitive drawing. The point to note from all these images is that the people who have 'drawn' them all work in a very different way under normal circumstances, a way that has been conditioned by their own life's journey. Drawing intuitively has allowed them to free themselves from the constriction and limitations of that path and some of the work they produce in this new environment is truly inspirational and often far outweighs what they have produced before.

In producing this work, they are presented with a visual expression of their own extraordinary capacities to create inspiring and visually exciting images, without the fear of failure or the need to conform to certain stereotypical styles. It is always enlightening.

[1] *Further details about John Hunter and the World Peace Game can be found at http://worldpeacegame.org .*

Visit **www.cultivating-intuition.com** *for more background, links to talks, images, references and a regular blog of new ideas.*

Part 2

The Eight Critical Questions

"It is always with excitement that I wake up in the morning wondering what my intuition will toss up to me, like gifts from the sea. I work with it and rely on it. It's my partner."

Jonas Salk, inventor of the Polio Vaccine

James Maberly

Intuitive drawing using charcoal and paint by Lesley Green

4

The Eight Critical Questions

It is less about DOING and more about BEING

We know that our intuition speaks to us on a regular basis. We also know that we have the capacity to develop those intuitive ideas into original concepts. What is less easy to explain is quite why it is that the majority of people don't ever take their original thoughts beyond this point.

The majority of us choose to work for someone else most of our lives. In the process, we rarely have the opportunity to follow our own dreams and desires, unless of course these fall into our leisure time activities. For some, working for someone else works well and if this is the case for you, then keep at it.

If however you are an original thinker and you are driven by a deep desire to follow your own dreams, then perhaps you need to think again.

In his book 'Screw Business As Usual'[1], Richard Branson began by saying;

"Over the last few decades as I've started up one exciting business after another, I thought that life and work could not get any better. In writing this book, I've realised that we've really been on a practise run, getting ready for the greatest challenge and opportunity of our lifetime. We've got a shot at really pulling together to turn upside down the way we approach the challenges we are facing in the world and look at them in a brand new entrepreneurial way. Never has there been a more exciting time for all of us to explore this great next frontier where the boundaries between work and purpose are merging into one, where doing good, really is good for business."

He inspires us to look at how we can do business in an entirely different way, to rethink how we look at the challenges we are facing. This requires new and original thought.

What follows are eight questions to consider that helped me to turn my original thoughts into reality. There is nothing fancy about any of them and they do not have catchy slogans to 'fit' with the latest management speak. In fact, they are less about DOING and more about BEING. There is an awful lot of literature out there about 'DOING', i.e. climbing up the ladder of success, yet in our pursuit of success it is often easy to separate our own personal values from the 'values' or 'ethos' of the organisation we work with. We are often happy to turn a blind eye to certain activities and perhaps, if we are the decision makers, to make certain decisions knowing that they are unethical and against accepted moral standards. Why do we do this? The question we should ask ourselves is 'how can we live with this conflicting duality'?

What Richard Branson is speaking of is exactly this – recognising that DOING is simply not good enough anymore. There is a huge consciousness shift taking place on the planet and people are beginning to stand up and fight for what they believe is right. They are no longer prepared to accept double standards. We see this in Europe and Africa and particularly in the Middle East. Both individual and corporate values now need to be working off the same song sheet.

As L.P. Hartley wrote, *"the past is a foreign country, they do things differently there"*[2]. It is time to move on. Today and in the future it is and will be much more about BEING. We need to bring 'ourselves' into the equation, the real 'us', hidden behind all the management speak, the bravado, the rules and the group think. Being ourselves is the key to the whole process. It is not always easy but once we have truly engaged with ourselves, everything becomes a whole lot easier. It really is time to move on.

I have been asking myself these questions over the last few years. They each convey specific areas that I have found challenging in my own life. Finding the time to deal with them in our busy schedules is not easy but the desire to consider them comes when we feel a genuine need to do so. Unlike schoolwork, no-one is telling us whether to consider these or not. It is entirely up to each of us individually and is very specific to our own journey.

The Eight Critical Questions are:

1) Whose rules are you following and why?
2) Do you really know who you are?
3) Do you have the courage to make mistakes openly?
4) Are you willing to embrace change?
5) Do you honestly trust yourself?
6) What is the tone of your communication with others?
7) Are you a 'true' or a selfish leader?
8) What is your passion?

May I suggest that you answer these questions for yourself first and then take time to read the corresponding chapters. I encourage you to question each chapter as much as you question yourself and to allow your intuition to help you sense where you stand in relation to each question. For me it has been about discovering a more enlightened way forward in which BEING takes centre stage and that I live life from a position of joy rather than fear and necessity.

---

[1] *From the introduction to 'Screw Business as Usual' by Richard Branson, Ebury 2011.*

[2] *Source; 'The Go-Between' by L.P. Hartley, published in 1953 by Hamish Hamilton.*

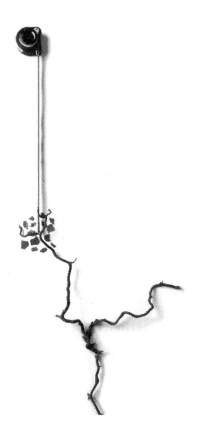

Intuitive drawing using found objects by Harry Maberly

5

Whose rules are you following and why?

**Our willingness to 'do what we're told' and
follow rules and conventions**

*"Do not believe what you have heard.
Do not believe in tradition because it has been handed down by
many generations.
Do not believe in anything that has been spoken many times.
Do not believe because the written statements come from some old
sage.
Do not believe in conjecture.
Do not believe in authority or teachers or elders.
But after careful observation and analysis, when it agrees with
reason and it will benefit one and all, then accept it and live by it."*
Buddha (Prince Siddhartha Gautama) 563 BC – 483 BC

On 19th December 2000, the BBC showed a documentary entitled
'5 Steps to Tyranny' produced and narrated by Sheena McDonald[1].
It was a deeply shocking film that clearly showed how those in
positions of power can cultivate the conditions for tyranny in any
population by demonstrating how easily ordinary people can be
manipulated into compliance with 'authority', into silence before
criminality and even how easily most ordinarily decent people
may be coerced into performing genuinely evil acts, evocative
of much that is happening in the world today. Her five steps are

listed below.

"To implement tyranny, the aspiring tyrant should undertake the following:

Level 1. 'Us' and 'them': use prejudice to foster the (fictional) notion of the existence of superior and dominant in-groups and inferior and powerless out-groups.
Level 2. Obey orders: insist that all people under your wing are to obey your orders.
Level 3. Dehumanize the enemy: emphasis on making inimical factions look less than human.
Level 4. 'Stand up' or 'stand by': suppress dissenting or opposing opinions to your own. (Suppression of all rebellion and dissenting opinion is the hallmark of tyranny.)
Level 5. Exterminate: be prepared to eliminate all those who are seen to pose a threat."

What the programme shows is that most of us are at level 1 in some way, whether it is divisions between Conservatives and Labour, Republicans and Democrats, rich and poor, working class and middle class, French and British, Islamic and Jewish, Catholics and Protestants or any other conflicting groups. Through clever manipulation of words, the 'authorities' can slide us into level 2 with a modicum of ease. Our acceptance of following orders and rules is well established at school and within other organisations in which we may participate and unwittingly we find it remarkably easy to allow ourselves to be guided along a sometimes unwelcome path. Whilst we know that there are many third world states that use coercion in various different ways to manipulate their populations, it is most certainly not only reserved to them. The US, British and other Governments used manipulation to create the atmosphere they most wanted after the 9/11 experience and greatly encouraged a level 3 view of Al Qaeda and later of the Iraqis by playing on the already angry, vulnerable and fearful populace, in the process developing extraordinary political mileage from it. It is remarkable to consider that one of the most advanced and democratic nations on earth could, even today, have encouraged people to be at level 3. There are many who still hold to that position and still vocalise it publically. It shows how fear can be manipulated by leaders to change any situation into one that suitably accommodates the actions they might wish to take.

'Group think' is another way, either manipulated by certain lead individuals or as a result of creeping 'contamination' in which people within a group take actions that they might not otherwise take and justify to themselves that it is in fact in their best interests (and perhaps of everyone else's) that they should do so. Religious zealots, autocrats, politicians and despots often use it. Don't however imagine it is restricted to them alone. We are all in a position to be affected and I am sure most of us have participated in some form of 'group think' at some stage of our lives.

At its most effective, it is a state of mind in which members of the 'group' fail to analyse critically and discuss adequately alternative courses of action. A classic example is when the British Government encouraged a 'perception' that Saddam Hussein's 'weapons of mass destruction' were at an advanced stage of development and that the nation had to act quickly. Even those in cabinet were so caught up in 'group think' that, despite consistent evidence to the contrary, they still agreed that the nation should go to war. So deep was the level of 'group think' that they even began to question the consistent evidence to the contrary before their eyes. Another example is the Challenger space shuttle disaster of 1986. Bloated with the confidence bred by previous successes, the senior management had a 'can't fail' approach to their launches. The launch had already been delayed four times and with added political pressure, they were determined that the launch should take place as soon as possible. Even when the experts were actively reporting to their superiors that the 'O' rings were defective and that the Challenger would explode if they were not replaced, they went ahead and launched anyway, with disastrous results.

In his book 'The Lucifer Effect', Philip Zimbardo creates empirical evidence about how easy it is for an ordinary group of people not only to become tyrannical but for others to accept and continue to participate in the roles of their victims without a fight. In fact so much so that the majority of the victims actually 'forgot' that they could walk out of the experiment at any stage.

His experiment involved a group of students who were randomly split into jailers and prisoners and placed in a simulated 'prison' in the Stanford University cellars. The jailers and the prisoners were each informed of the roles they had to play in the simulation, which was supposed to last for 3 weeks. Within 5 days it had escalated into a situation so completely barbaric and out of hand that they had to call the whole experiment off.

Similar experiments relating to obedience to authority figures were carried out by Yale University psychologist Stanley Milgram between 1961 and 1974 with equally surprising results.

Where do you stand?

This evidence can be profoundly shocking to read and it is disturbing to recognise that we can be manipulated so easily into doing things that we do not intend or even wish to do. Yet, this is happening to us all the time and most of the time we are completely unaware of it. It often happens very subtly. This can easily be recognised by our adherence to the 'fashion' of the day, be it the latest fashionable wear or the fact that wearing a suit and tie is the 'norm' for the office. Men tend to wear fairly drab outfits to dinner parties (black tie) whilst women dress up. Why is that? In nature it is often the males who have the most delightful displays and in the days of the cavaliers, the men dressed up as brightly and as lavishly as the women.

At home, many families have 'rules' about, for example, where things should be put and how to behave, who should do what and when. These 'rules' establish boundaries for the growing family and are very important in the development of the individual. Clearly though there are some who take this to extremes and for some men (and women) the home is a place where they can command control in a way that they might not be able to do elsewhere, satisfying a personal need which instead of enabling the child, does exactly the opposite.

In most schools, rules are laid out for the direction of both staff and pupils. These provide a 'template' on which the school operates and allows a structure within which pupils can feel 'safe'. The very best schools nowadays use the rules more as a guidance system than as a rigid format. Whilst there are certain activities which quite rightly need to be 'policed' carefully, it is the ability of the headmaster and the staff to be flexible in how they deal with issues that come up which determines how the youngsters in their care will perceive the issue of control. For younger children, rules are firmer to ensure the boundaries provide a safe environment. As pupils enter their final years of school the best schools relax these rules, allowing pupils to explore and start to recognise the need to set up internal boundaries for themselves. Some schools even encourage debate amongst these elder pupils on the whole concept of control, thus encouraging them to consider their positions and to learn to set their own boundaries. Regrettably there are not enough schools doing this yet.

Schools of course follow structured systems; all over the world, systems of education have been developed based on what academics and the hierarchy believe to be the correct standards and the right way forward. The current public education system was developed to educate youngsters in the 19th Century for the needs of Industrialism. What we have today is based solidly on that model. A question that has been raised in recent years by many learned people is, 'is it still fit for purpose'?

Jacob Barnett[2], a young man in the USA with an IQ of 189 (who at 14 is studying Quantum Mechanics at Indiana University-Purdue University, Indianapolis) recently threw his opinion into the ring. Through his research he has come to realise that it was not genius that provided such people as Isaac Newton and Albert Einstein with their great discoveries and theories. Rather, it was their break from 'regular' education, allowing them time to think for themselves, unrestrained by set patterns and it was in this 'free space' that their greatest creative moments occurred. His cry to other young teenagers is '..you're doing it all wrong. Stop learning and start thinking for yourselves'. He argues that there are many people with very high IQ's but few of them follow their own paths to discovery.

His mother withdrew him from the standard educational and special needs system completely at the age of three and has said that rather than directing him, she has always followed his interests and thus allowed him to expand in those areas that interested him. This is certainly a very different way of providing an education but when so many capable and creative youngsters are diagnosed with such conditions as ADHD and are 'medicated' in order to fit into a normal learning environment, perhaps we need to ask ourselves why we feel the need to make them 'fit' into our world? What makes us think we are right? What if we placed them in a different environment and took a different approach? Is it not perhaps time to review the rules and our motives?

Reprinted with kind permission of John L. Hart FLP.[3]

Most religions have pretty solid structures around how worshipers should or should not behave. Most would deny they were rules, suggesting that they are merely 'guidelines' but it is difficult for anyone wishing to be a regular participant not to follow the guidelines as if they are rules. Historically leaders have used religion for the purposes of control. This does not in any way suggest that the spiritual messages given are wrong, just that the way the man-made and managed religious institutions themselves have been used with ulterior motives. One only has to look at the history of the Jewish, Christian, Islamic, Hindu and Shinto religions (to name but a few) to recognise that they have often been used to incite extreme action against others 'in the name of God or Gods'.

Incidentally, when both sides are saying the war is 'in the name of God', which one is right? I wonder sometimes whether the Jewish, Christian and Islamic religions have forgotten that they have one aspect in common which perhaps they need to revisit and explore more fully; Abraham is the father of them all. He is the uniting factor and it is Abraham's God that they all worship. Isn't that therefore the same God?   No !

One very obvious separation in perceptions created by religious beliefs are those in relation to sexuality and the human body. In Christianity, the human body has always been seen as a potential hotbed of sin. Our natural desires for sexual interaction with others are considered sinful and shameful. More than that, we were born in sin. Augustine of Hippo and the Coptic Monks informed us that it was only by mortifying the body and fighting off temptations of the flesh that one could attain perfection. Even today, books are still being written by religious writers encouraging strict controls over the mind and body in order to achieve a state of happiness. These beliefs have infused western cultures to such an extent that a high percentage of those who are not religious still hold to these underlying beliefs.

To the Buddhists and Hindus it was very different. There was no association of women or sexuality with sin. Women were associated with fertility, prosperity and abundance: in fact, sexuality was seen as supremely divine. The walls of their monasteries were decorated with images of attractively voluptuous women and copulating couples. Today, because of the influence of Christian

Missionaries and British educated Hindu reformers, Hindu women have been forced to take a more 'Christian' approach to their bodies and their sexuality.

The question is not whether one is right and the other is wrong (that argument could go on for ever): rather it is whether we can loosen ourselves enough from the anchors of our own conditioning to accept that they each present valid ways of seeing the roles of men and women and of sexuality which may be completely different to our own. It is just another set of rules.

The issue of sexual orientation itself raises serious debate across the globe. Generally, homosexuality is seen as 'wrong' and an 'aberration'. Most religions and many cultures have strong anti-homosexual attitudes and those who are gay or lesbian feel marginalised. It is often assumed that they are making a choice to be so and that with a little 'help and guidance', they could be reoriented back to 'normality'.

Those who are gay or lesbian will tell you that there is no choice in the matter – it is the way they are. It is natural: it is a state of being. The only choice is in whether they choose to act on their natural inclinations or whether they should deny them. Nor is homosexuality new: it has been with us for as long as recorded history.

So which set of rules and guidelines do we choose to follow, one that excludes or one that accepts? Is it conditioned by what makes us feel safe? Are all gay people inherently suspicious or wrong or is this simply a myth encouraged by our assimilated fear of change and difference or perhaps the conventions of our religion or upbringing?

All of the rules and perceptions we hold have foundations in our childhood. Changing them is not easy but if we are to truly engage with our intuitive selves, we need to consider where we stand and make our own choices, rather than simply following the rules and conventions of society.

Why Follow Rules?

John Bradshaw

John Bradshaw lives in Zimbabwe. When he completed his schooling in 1978 he was called up for national service in the Rhodesian army and was assigned to a mine detection unit. Whilst disarming a booby-trapped land mine one day it exploded and John received severe injuries to his hands and face. As a result, he lost the sight in one eye and no longer had full vision in the other.

For any young person about to launch into their adult life such an experience, together with the resulting disability, could be devastating. What was he to do? How would he manage? How would he earn a living?

Although John was an intelligent young man he had performed below his potential at school. He was extremely shy and very reticent in putting himself forward. He was constrained in his thinking, primarily as a consequence of his narrow world view but also by his reluctance to seek advice. His parents encouraged him to follow certain directions which they felt would safely provide him with a satisfying job and a good income.

The accident changed everything. As he came to terms with his injuries he realised that he was not constrained in the ways in which he had previously thought. The perceived expectations of his parents and others around him had disappeared. The conversations which he now had with others were different. He had survived an explosion which by rights should have killed him instantly, and as a result everyone was simply delighted that he was still alive. He realised that there were no longer expectations as no-one, including him, could anticipate what would be possible in the future.

With such uncertainties and without the old perceived constraints, John could have fallen into depression and inactivity. However, without anyone trying to guide him in any specific direction and no rules to follow, he realised that he was free to do exactly what he wished. He could literally choose any direction he wanted and everyone would be pleased with whatever he managed to achieve. He was liberated in a way that he had never experienced before. But what was he to do?

John took the time to listen to his intuition and recognise what it was he truly wanted to do. He took the plunge and went on to study for a PhD at Cambridge University.

Over time his eyesight disappeared completely and he is now totally blind. Yet despite this obvious handicap, John today holds the post of Headmaster of Peterhouse Girls in Zimbabwe, one of the elite senior private schools in the country. He is the only blind person at the school and is, as far as I am aware, the only totally blind person running a regular school anywhere in the world.

Everything we do and every attitude we have is a personal choice

The majority of us are, whether we realise it or not, following rules. The real independent thinkers amongst us are those who have for the most part set their own rules, their own boundaries. They are able to 'fit with the crowd' when they need to but can be completely independent of it if they so choose. Very few of us fit into this category but when we come across these people, they stand out from the crowd. The point to learn from these people is that they understand that rules abound around them but they choose whether they wish to follow them or not and for how long. They are governed by their own internal boundaries and structures and not by external ones. They could be described as 'sovereign' beings. Abraham Maslow, the author of 'Toward a Psychology of Being' described them as fully 'self-actualised' people[4].

If we go back to the start of the chapter and read the quote from Buddha, he challenges us to think hard before we accept anything as truth. Nothing is sacred. Everything should be considered carefully before we decide it is worth adopting or not. We should ask questions, do our homework and above all, trust our intuitive feelings about it. They will often give us a strong sense of 'knowing' when a certain path is right or wrong. Following a certain direction just because our friends, family or peers do so is a clear indication that we are not yet listening to and responding to our own inner voice. There comes a time when we need to move beyond that and make our own choices, independent of the influence of others.

Whether we believe it or indeed like it or not, we are already choosing our own responses to everything we do, though often allowing ourselves to be heavily influenced by others. For example, if we feel that someone has 'pressured' us into doing something we don't really wish to do, we tend to blame the fact on them. The reality is that we have actually made the choice to 'allow' that influence, so there is no one to blame. Sadly a culture has developed within our society, ably assisted by the press and the legal fraternity, which encourages us to apportion blame to others for our 'unfortunate' circumstances, perpetuating the view that what is happening is entirely out of our control. What we should more sensibly do is recognise our own part in this process, learn from the experience and move on: that would be creative and would move us forward.

If I believe in something very deeply, then that becomes the energy and vibration I give off and as a consequence I am rewarded with more of what I believe. For example, if I believe that the world is a terrible place, everyone is against me and I am surrounded by evil-minded bullies, then that is what I see and that is how I am affected. That becomes my chronic point of attraction and evidence of it constantly pops out at me to justify my perceptions. Thus I am right and I can prove it. I literally focus it into being.

Yet if I believe that the world is an exciting place to live and is changing for the better and that what is happening around me is all evidence of that adjustment, the proof I need for this perception will be revealed to me constantly, which of course proves I am unquestionably right.

Which of these approaches do I choose? Which feels most comfortable? Both are right (after all, the confirmation is there) but would I prefer to live my life in joy or in misery?

If we think of animals for a moment, we see an interesting life process occurring. Unless animals are unwell or kept in restrictive conditions by humans, for the most part they live joyous lives. They hop, skip and play, eat and have babies. If they get a fright, they scatter and if they are caught, they die but once the threat has gone the others are back, hopping, skipping and playing once more. What we don't see are groups of animals sitting around being miserable, gazing into the distance and cradling bottles of Grouse whisky. Is there a lesson to be learnt from this?

If my daughter JoJo goes off to hockey practise complaining that it will be dreadful, there is surely no surprise when it is! She recently went off to her County Girls Cricket team selection day with a bounce in her step and a twinkle in her eye and played brilliantly, resulting in her being selected for the team. In both cases, she focused her resultant actions into being.

Government, Institutional control and unexpected events

There are of course things that 'happen' to us, whether through Government action, Institutional action or an event (such as a torrential storm or a fuel shortage). Quite how we respond to these happenings is actually entirely up to us and that is what makes all the difference. Each will affect us to a greater or lesser degree but if we see ourselves as victims, we are disempowered. We could easily become immersed in all the feelings of bitterness and anger surrounding the event and affect our on-going lives as a result. Or we could choose differently.

A family I know in Zimbabwe who were farmers had a son who, owing to an injury to his neck during the Rhodesian war, became a quadriplegic. His mother accepted it (as he did – and what a remarkable man he became) and moved on but his father remained embittered. Later, the family were driven off their farm by invaders and lost everything. Of course everyone was angry at first, but the mother and son put it behind them. The father became more and more deeply embittered, spending his days picking holes in everything he saw and read. He died not long afterwards, his body unable to take the debilitating toxins he was creating as a result of his constant rage and bitterness.

How does Intuition fit into this?

Intuition is being fed to us constantly. If, because of our adherence to certain rules or beliefs we do not allow ourselves the privilege of listening to it, no benefit will be gained. Equally if we listen but do not allow ourselves the privilege of doing anything with it, then clearly nothing creative or original will occur. Many people go through life convinced for some reason that they are not capable of thinking up or doing anything creative or original.

Ego is generally the motivator behind the desire to be 'a part of the group', to be seen to be 'someone' or indeed to play the role of the victim. We can be very strongly influenced by those opinions or 'truths' that have become firmly 'pegged' in our minds, which feed the ego with its core food. The more we are able to separate ourselves from the ego and relax into our intuitive selves (see Chapter 6), the easier it will become to set our own rules and guidelines and become independent of the other rules around us. The more we do that, the easier it will be to allow our intuitive ideas to take seed and formulate new and creative ways ahead – in our own individual way.

"Any fool can make a rule, and any fool will mind it."
Henry David Thoreau (1817-1862)

"It is the death of the spirit we must fear. To believe only what one is taught and brought up to believe, to repeat what one has been told to say, to do only what one is expected to do, to live like a factory made doll, to lose confidence in one's independence and the hope of better things – that is the death of the spirit."
Tokutomi Roka – Japanese author. Died 1927

41

[1] *On 19th December 2000, the BBC showed a documentary entitled '5 Steps to Tyranny' produced and narrated by Sheena McDonald. It remains a classic and can be viewed on Youtube and Vimeo.*

[2] *BC is reprinted with permission of John L. Hart FLP. It is produced by John Hart Studios. Their website is at www.johnhartstudios.com*

[3] *Jacob Barnett is an American teenager with an IQ of 189, currently studying for a Master's Degree in Quantum Mechanics at the age of 14. He recently gave a TED talk which can be seen on the book website at www.cultivating-intuition.com which explains his ideas about education.*

[4] *Self-Actualized people tend to accept themselves and others as they are. They tend to lack inhibition and are able to enjoy themselves and their lives free of guilt. Other people are treated the same regardless of background, current status or other socio-economic and cultural factor.*
Kendra Cherry – www.about.com

6

Do you really know who you are?

The egoical self and the intuitive self

"Each of you acquires opinions and beliefs about yourself during your upbringing. You absorb ideas and images from your parents, family, peers, school, etc. You begin to play certain roles without questioning them, and you soon develop something called a 'personality': a set of habits, behaviours, and thoughts. But at some time in the course of growing up, something else awakens in you. First, it is no more than a whisper; a memory that you cannot place; a knowing that you are more than what is just determined by the world outside yourself. There is something deeper, a layer that cannot be contained and understood by the human intellect. Herein lies your core, that which precedes and survives the earthly sphere – your soul."

Pamela Kribbe – Aurelia (www.jeshua.net)

The title question has been occupying the minds of philosophers, theologists and psychoanalysts for many years. People sometimes spend their whole lives looking at very specific aspects of this and come up with a mass of data which proves or disproves certain points. All of this is relevant and useful and can be really helpful in solving very specific problems and recommending certain practices but it often gets to the point where one can no longer see the wood for the trees.

In a world in which we are bombarded with information from all sides, it is easy to assume that we are over informed and that we are taxing our mental capacities constantly. We might appear to have extended our abilities to hold information, but I would

43

argue that whether we live in the jungle in Borneo or work in the UN in New York, we are constantly receiving and processing information all of the time. We have an extraordinary capacity for gathering data and we have sensors that are constantly doing this every moment of the day in many forms, the most obvious of which are sight, sound, touch, taste and smell. Much of this will be subconsciously happening almost as a peripheral view but is all-accessible to us at a later stage if we need it. I would argue that all we have done is adjusted some of the information we are receiving and made more of it 'conscious information' than it was before.

Information though is not really the issue here. We already know that our minds and bodies are capable of gathering and processing information. We need to recognise that by willingly listening to our intuition, we can creatively use this gathered information to enhance everything we do.

So, what stops us? We have touched on the ego and how it has such an extraordinary power over us, literally pulling our strings so effectively that we are responding like dancing puppets. Let us consider this power a little more.

The egoical self and its components

Most people tend to believe that the mind and the ego are intertwined and that they are inseparable. It is easy to accept this as almost every interaction in which we participate and in every response we have to events, we tend to involve both facets at the same time.

The fact is they are completely separate parts of our makeup. The mind is a very useful tool and when put to good use it is exceptionally valuable, as can be seen by our progress into the modern age of technology. The ego on the other hand is a survival mechanism. It allows us to establish an identity but is directly affected by inputs we process every day. The basis of our egoical responses is formed as a consequence of the many and varied inputs we have had over the years.

Alan McLean is a Glasgow based Psychologist who works closely with the Scottish Government on various educational advisory councils. He has written two books of note. In his book 'The Motivated School' (2003), he considered what it was that motivated or de-motivated children. *"In my research, I have been amazed over and over again at how quickly students of all ages pick up on messages about themselves – at how sensitive they are to suggestions about their personal qualities or about the meaning of their actions and experiences. The kinds of praise (and criticism) students receive from their teachers and parents tell them how to think about what they do – and what they are."* [1]

Carol Dweck is the Lewis and Virginia Eaton Professor of Psychology at Stanford University. She is widely regarded as one of the world's leading researchers in the fields of personality, social psychology, and developmental psychology. Over many years, she has been conducting surveys on motivation and personality which includes research into our responses to praise and criticism and has written several books: 'Self-Theories' in 1999 and 'Mindset: The New Psychology of Success' in 2006. In this, she suggests that the type of mind-set we hold throughout our lives (which unfolds primarily in childhood and continues to develop into adulthood) drives every aspect of our lives. She also suggests we can change our mind-set at any stage in life to undertake whatever it is we wish to achieve.

Her work has been closely followed by Carol Craig, herself an author of three books on the subject of well-being and who is Chief Executive of the 'Centre for Confidence and well-being' in Glasgow, Scotland. She had the following to say about Dweck's work.

'Dweck (argues) that praising for high achievement often carries a big risk....her research suggests that when children are praised for how intelligent they are, they become focused on retaining this label rather than on continuing to learn. Dweck argues praise for intelligence often leads children to become more interested in

how they are seen by others than in the learning itself. So praising for intelligence, or talent, may seem a positive thing to do but can distort children's attitude to learning and get them dependent on how they are seen by others. In practice this can mean not opting for challenging tasks or trying new things if it might involve failure'. [2]

Based on this, the following examples demonstrate to us how the ego can affect us all (and particularly children as they grow up) and how we are very much at its mercy.

a) Give praise for, say, intelligence to someone and the ego will instantly respond by encouraging the recipient to see themselves as 'special' and thus a 'status' is established *for themselves* and also in relation to others around them.

b) It instantly introduces the concept of fear – 'if I do something that might show I am not as intelligent as she said I am, then I might look a fool, not only to others *but also to myself*, so I better think carefully before I do that'. As a consequence, the pupil may not risk answering a question publically if they are unsure of the answer and perhaps even if they do know, just in case they are wrong.

You will note that I have introduced two points in *italics* which I feel are equally (if not more) important. I believe it doesn't just extend to what other people might think of us; it will affect the way we think about ourselves and the last thing we want to do is damage our own self-perception, whether influenced by others or not. If this egoical perception were to be further encouraged, so the fear of failure would rise also and a need to be seen to be 'intelligent' may become a fixation. At a glance this may seem to be harmless but it may then encourage 'protection mechanisms' such as arrogance or a determination to look good 'at all costs'. This is where the ego can start to play unpleasant games in an effort to ensure its safety. The point is that the ego is essentially 'self-centred'. It is interested in itself first and will do anything to ensure it stays centre stage in our lives.

The filter

Every day, a myriad of inputs and opinions enter our conscious minds which relate directly to us. Multiply these opinions (i.e. 'I am intelligent' and 'I don't want to look a fool') millions of times and you begin to get a picture of how many different inputs we have over our lifetimes that directly affect the way we see and think about ourselves.

As we grow up we hear and feel how our parents and siblings react and respond to everything. The same goes for our teachers, friends, television, radio, the news, books we read, the films we watch and much, much more. We are also constantly aware of our own involvement in everything we participate in and we judge our own abilities based on the reactions around us and by comparing ourselves with others. All this information pours into our minds and directly affects the way we see and place ourselves within society.

I would like to simplify this concept by making it more graphic and thus easier to comprehend. Imagine that when you are born, an ephemeral board (a bit like a chessboard) floats beside you full of holes, ready for pegs to be slotted into them. The size of the board is small at first but will extend as your life proceeds. As each experience happens in your life which has a direct affect/impact on you, a peg goes into the board and written on the peg is a label. For example in the beginning it would be feelings i.e. fear, anxiety, joy, pain, anger.

As you progress through life, the pegs are made up of all those experiences you have of your own or those of others around you at home, school, the playground, church, sport etc. They become more specific. For example, I am good at football, I am bad at maths, I am shy, Mr Jones says I am stupid, I am naughty, I am clever, John says am ugly, the PE teacher says I am useless, I am funny etc. After a while, there are certain pegs that are reinforced

47

constantly by others around us and indeed by ourselves and they become 'pillars' of our self-perception. By the time we are 18 years old, millions and millions of inputs have earned a place on our board, which has grown somewhat in size.

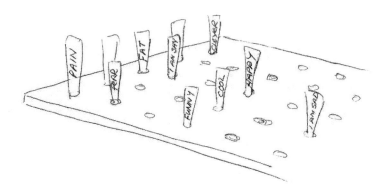

Now imagine that this board shrinks and slots into the back of your head wherein it takes the role of being a filter. Every piece of information that now enters your mind, whatever it is, has first to pass through this filter. Thus how we respond to that information once it reaches our mind will depend entirely on what our filter is guiding us to do. That filter, which forms the basis of our egoical selves, has extraordinary power. So for example, even though you know the answer to the question being asked by the teacher at the front of the class, your experience of 'getting it wrong' and 'being picked on for being stupid' in the past may guide you to keep your hand down, rather than potentially expose yourself to another blast of ridicule in the playground later if you are wrong.

A large percentage of the information 'written' on these pegs is not of our own creation, especially that derived from the comments of others. We have simply decided to 'own' these opinions and thus allow them to affect us. Once they are on the board, we see them as 'truth'. We believe and live our lives by them and they have the power to heavily influence the compasses we set for our lives ahead.

Certain judgements are reinforced by other people, sometimes cruelly, but mostly they are reinforced by us. We are our own fiercest critics and in our low moments, the pegs that are most reinforced stand out like beacons, reminding us of our debilitating 'weaknesses'. They can even become the basis for some of our core beliefs (see chapter 9). Of course for some it can work in the other direction, i.e. people who are very beautiful, exceptional sports players, film stars or popular musicians may become overconfident, selfish and egotistical, believing they are infallible.

Of course none of this is set in stone. Not only are the majority of these pegs just plain wrong, they can be changed. So in fact each one could be removed, examined and considered carefully from a 'helicopter perspective', the label scraped off and a new label written on the peg. It does however take an extraordinarily long time.

Henri Nouwen[3], a Dutch priest, theologian, psychologist and noted author of 40 books who lectured at both Yale and Harvard, broke our everyday lives down into three categories:

a) We are what we achieve - i.e. work, sport, drama etc. In other words we base our value as individuals on external activities.

b) We are what other people think of us - Often the most powerful driver. When we are popular or liked, we feel secure. When we are unpopular or not even noticed, then we feel very vulnerable and depressed.

c) We are what we 'own' – property, education, health, family. So dependant do we generally become on these that if we lose them, we feel extremely vulnerable and it might affect our state of mind. They become 'anchors' in our lives.

He explains that as a result of our dependence on these egoical viewpoints, our life graphs tend to move in a zigzag from start to finish. He goes on to explain that this perception of our lives is all wrong. It is a survival mechanism which we have allowed to dominate our sense of self. We can therefore choose not to be controlled by the ego and in the process discover something remarkable about ourselves which we already know but don't seem to recognise and thus take no notice of; the intuitive self.

The Intuitive Self

Charles Handy[4] at the opening of his autobiography 'Myself and Other More Important Matters' had this wonderful anecdote to relate which clearly speaks of his own journey to reconcile himself with who he really is.

"Some years ago I was helping my wife arrange an exhibit of her photographs of Indian tea gardens when I was approached by a man who had been looking at the pictures. 'I hear that Charles Handy is here,' he said. 'Indeed he is,' I replied, 'and I am he.' He looked at me rather dubiously for a moment, and then said, 'Are you sure?' It was, I told him, a good question because over time there had been many versions of Charles Handy, not all of which I was particularly proud."

I recall at the age of thirty saying to a close friend of mine, "I am taking some time off to try and 'find' myself'". I had just had a rather earth-shattering experience in my life and was feeling somewhat shaken by it. I recall he looked at me rather blankly and said "what is it that you are hoping to find?" I don't remember my answer, but I recall his question and it has often crossed my mind since then. It was a phrase much used twenty years ago as people searched desperately for something in themselves that would give them comfort or direction or a sense of identity.

The concept of 'finding oneself' suggests searching for something. During that period of time I read many books on psychology, on positive thinking and books on how to mimic great people and take on their attributes. I read Viktor Frankl's book 'Man's search for Meaning'[5] about his experiences in Auschwitz.

Frankl questioned whether man was simply a product of his environment, inescapably influenced by his surroundings. He determined that man does have a choice and that he can maintain a spiritual freedom and an independence of mind despite whatever circumstances prevail. That was the first time I began to recognise that there was nothing to search for – that it was inherent within us already and we simply needed to climb down from the rooftop into the calm interior and there we would find it all.

"We who lived in the concentration camps can remember the men who walked through the huts comforting others, giving away their last piece of bread. They may have been few in number, but they offer sufficient proof that everything can be taken from a man but one thing: The last of his freedoms – to choose one's attitude in any given set of circumstances, to choose one's own way."
Viktor Frankl, 'Man's Search for Meaning', Beacon Press, 1959

For most of those inmates, daily life must have been quite appalling. Some simply lost the will to live. Young strong muscular men with seemingly positive attitudes just gave up and within weeks, sometimes even days, they died. Their happiness (or lack of it) was based on the external, what they could or could not do for themselves or for others. They were dominated by their own egoical perceptions. Yet those people whom Frankl speaks of in the quotation above were living in the same conditions, the same dreadful circumstances. What was it that they had discovered that made all the difference to them?

I suggest that they had stopped searching, stopped comparing their lives to others or what they could or should be and discovered the intuitive self, that quiet space inside, unaffected by the drama that surrounded them. Here they recognised the beauty and pleasure of being themselves and recognised their ability to think of and appreciate their lives differently. They made the choice to shift from the egoical perception (with all the drama) to the peaceful intuitive perception, and that made all the difference.

Frankl refers to it as 'the last of (man's) freedoms'. I would like to re-write this and say it is the most important of man's freedoms - the trouble is, we simply don't realise it and our experiences in life (and those of everyone around us) give no indication that the choice exists.

The intuitive self works very differently to the ego. It feels into the energy all around us, using all of our senses. We both give off and receive energy from everything around us all the time and the intuitive self responds to this. It is not affected in any way by the filter. It also listens to the intellect and quietly responds to everything that is happening, acting like a second, but much quieter mind. If we do not hear it speaking to us it is because we have either blocked it (usually because we have been educated out of giving it any credibility) or the noise of the ego is so loud we cannot hear it. It has no investment in staking its claim over us (as the ego does) and so often goes completely unnoticed.

Seeing the bigger picture

So how do we find the intuitive self? The ego has a very strong grip on our thought patterns and so until we recognise the difference between them, it is difficult to know when we are consciously listening to the intuitive self. The intuitive self is very quiet.

The most effective way I have discovered to help release myself from the hold of the ego when I am becoming frustrated or fearful over something (when my ego is in full swing) is to take three or four deep breaths (and more if I need to). It seems to create a 'space' between my ego and me and I am able to see the egoical reaction from a 'helicopter' perspective and by that I mean I can 'look' at it from a distance. At this point I often experience two trains of thought at exactly the same time. The first is the loud egoical response often full of emotion, frustration, judgement, fear and/or anger whilst the second is quiet, peaceful, unaffected and non-judgemental and generally suggests a very sensible way forward. This is the intuitive self, the quiet central point in me that has no investment in fighting for my position, defending me, chastising me or dominating others. It is content. Here is the moment that I release the egoical response and respond to the quieter voice. It is always a wonderfully calming and revealing moment.

The 'Zone'

Actors, singers, paramedics, firemen and many others speak of an extraordinary place they 'go' to when under intense pressure, when emotions and the ego are being stretched to their full capacity. They refer to it as the 'Zone'. In that space everything calms down, worries subside, they feel in complete control and they are able to concentrate on what it is they are doing with an ease that is unencumbered by the restraints of ego. This is a perfect example of working from the intuitive self.

Everyone is likely to have experienced this in some way (even if they don't recognise it as such). Most of the time, unlike the 'Zone' described above, our everyday lives are conducted in much less intense scenarios and yet the intuitive self and this space are accessible at all times. To live it more regularly and naturally it does require a little transition and here are four stages to help you guide your progress along the way.

1. Being unsatisfied by what ego based consciousness has to offer you, longing for 'something else'.

2. Becoming aware of your ties to ego based consciousness, recognizing and releasing the emotions and thoughts that go with it.

3. Letting the old ego based energies inside you die, throwing off the cocoon, becoming your intuitive self.

4. The awakening of a heart based consciousness within you,

motivated by love and freedom and helping others make the transition to the same place.[6]

In these two truly delightful poems below (from the Gitanjali), Rabindranath Tagore[7] (winner of the Nobel Prize for literature in 1913) describes his ego from a 'helicopter' perspective, showing that even he found difficulty in shaking himself loose from it. Tagore clearly recognised the intuitive self and the fact that it is our inner core (he refers to it as the true being) and was deeply aware of how strong the pull of ego was and the vast difference between the two.

Song 29
"He whom I enclose with my name is weeping in this dungeon. I am ever busy building this wall all around; and as this wall goes up into the sky day by day I lose sight of my true being in its dark shadow.
I take pride in this great wall, and I plaster it with dust and sand lest a hole should be left in this name; and for all the care I take I lose sight of my true being."

Song 30
"I came out alone on my way to my tryst. But who is this that follows me in the silent dark?
I move aside to avoid his presence but I escape him not.
He makes the dust rise from the earth with his swagger; he adds his loud voice to every word that I utter.
He is my own little self, my lord, he knows no shame; but I am ashamed to come to thy door in his company."

Rabindranath Tagore (1861 – 1941) Gitanjali

For some, responding to their intuition is easy as they have not encumbered themselves with 'limitations' to stop them and thus freely utilise this extraordinary resource. For others of us (and I include myself in this group until I realised otherwise), deep in our filter are blocks created both by external influences and by our own personal criticisms of self. Once the pegs are set in place, we simply respond to them. For most of us, the fear of making a fool of ourselves in front of others is enough to stop us dead in our tracks. We will find any excuse to justify our actions. For example, 'I haven't got the time', 'my kids need my focus', 'it wouldn't fit with my work' etc. The fact is, we are afraid to try.

So how do we start? How do we engage?

Create something, but don't spend too much time thinking about it. Too much thought kills creativity whilst intuition brings it to life. Just the very act of creating something, whether it is a drawing, an arrangement of flowers, re-arranging a room or building a Lego house frees you to tap into your intuition more actively. Just create for the sake of creating. No more.

Meditation is good, as is lying quietly in the bath and another excellent way to place yourself into an environment for creative thought is to take a walk. As you walk, take several deep breaths and try and separate yourself from the incessant chatter in your mind. Look around you. Feel into the beauty around you, the sky, the sunset and the colours. Engage with it and breathe it in. The space created will allow for a calmer and quieter mind, allowing easier access to the intuitive self.

Steve Jobs, unless he was for some reason unable to do so, always took those with whom he was meeting for a walk. Why? It was because his mind was at its most creative and open whilst he was walking. My son Harry, when deep in thought, walks in anticlockwise circles around the kitchen table. At school he used to rock in his chair, much to the frustration of his teachers. Why? He needs to move to think. Gillian Lynne, the world-renowned ballet dancer and choreographer was the same. It is movement that frees them to engage their most creative thought.

The egoical self is generally our default mechanism. For most of us it has been so all our lives and it does tend to dominate our perception of who we are and where we fit in the grand scheme of things. Whilst the ego is an important part of our makeup, it is only a part. It is a survival mechanism and a useful tool, an add-on, a bit like a computer 'app'. It is a tool we can make use of. Allowing the ego to ride roughshod over us all the time is a bit like letting the tail wag the dog.

The intuitive self is our core, our centre. The intuitive self has full access to all our capabilities, senses and assets of which the ego is one (when used sensibly). We just need to learn how to keep it in its place. What needs to change is our dependence on it. We need to be independent of it, choosing to use its extraordinary facets as and when we need to. That way it becomes an asset and not a liability. When we listen to the intuitive self, we are not constricted by the filter. We by-pass it completely, freeing us from its often debilitating limitations.

Often when challenges arise, we try and think our way out of them and this sometimes ends up with the issue spiralling around and around in our minds, many a time without solution. When this next happens, step away from your desk (or wherever you are), take a walk and breathe. Concentrate for a moment on the act of breathing and allow yourself to calm down, freeing your mind from the chatter. Permit your intuition to drop ideas in on how to solve it. It might not happen instantly but the more you free yourself from the incessant chatter, the easier it is to hear the intuitive 'voice'. You will surprise yourself with your ability to reconsider the issues. Be persistent and you will slowly begin to see life through different eyes.

[1] Alan McLean – quote from 'The Motivated School' published in 2003 by Sage.

[2] *Carol Craig- The 'Centre for Confidence and Well-being' - www. centreforconfidence.co.uk*

[3] *Henri Nouwen travelled widely and spoke often of our dependence on the external aspects of our lives. He died on September 21, 1996. Nouwen's books are still being read today. His books include The Wounded Healer, In the Name of Jesus, Clowning in Rome, The Life of the Beloved and The Way of the Heart. After nearly two decades of teaching at the Menninger Foundation Clinic in Topeka, Kansas, and at the University of Notre Dame, Yale University and Harvard University, he went to work with mentally challenged people at the L'Arche community of Daybreak in Toronto, Canada.(Wikipedia)*

[4] *Charles Handy is an author and philosopher who has published 19 books. He is a specialist in organisational behaviour and management. The quote is from his book 'Myself and other more important matters' published by Arrow in 2006.*

[5] *Victor Frankl (1905 – 1997) was an Austrian neurologist and psychiatrist as well as a Holocaust survivor. Frankl was the founder of Logotherapy, 'Man's search for Meaning' was his most successful book.*

[6] *Pamela Kribbe – Aurelia (www.jeshua.net)*

[7] *Rabindranath Tagore (7 May 1861 – 7 August 1941) was a Bengali polymath who reshaped his region's literature and music. Author of the Gitanjali, he became the first non-European to win the Nobel Prize in Literature in 1913.*

James Maberly

Intuitive drawing using found objects

7

Do you have the courage to make mistakes openly?

The fear of messing up

I sat at the front of the talk waiting to be told what my role would be in the up and coming negotiation. I was attending an Advanced Negotiation course at Kent University in the UK. This particular simulated negotiation was to take at least four hours with a two-hour preparation period before the negotiation began. I had two distinct feelings running through me: the first was that I really wanted to do this as communication between races is one of my areas of deep interest and I knew that we had French, Russian, Chinese, Thai and Dutch participants in the negotiation to follow.

The second was a debilitating fear of participating in any way whatsoever. I could feel the tension rising in my back and I could feel my tongue already drying up in my mouth. This had often happened before in such scenarios and up until then I had simply dealt with it. As my father used to say, "Just buckle down and get on with it. Don't let the fear get in your way".

Today I paused and asked myself, 'why am I so damned scared? Here I am, over 50 years old and still sweating – this is ridiculous! What the hell is driving this fear?' My thoughts ran to fear of failure, fear of looking a fool in front of my peers, fear of looking a fool in front of my tutor, fear of making the wrong decisions altogether.

As I brooded over this, I suddenly remembered two quotes, both of which I had taken notice of in times past. The first was a quote I had read and reflected on some years previously:

"When I reach the next world, they will not ask me why I was not Moses. They will ask me why I was not Zuzya".

Rabbi Zuzya of Hannipol

The second was one I had heard in a sermon given some years ago by Henri Nouwen.

"I never realised that broken glass could shine so brightly."

The fact that they had just slipped into my mind right then was none other than my intuition nudging me, feeding me with my next source of wisdom at exactly the moment I needed it. As I considered this, everything began to fall quietly into place. It all made complete sense. It was a bit like watching a line of dominoes all colliding and crashing down in sequence.

A great friend of mine once said to me in jest "I have only ever made one mistake in my life and that was on 27th January 1972". It was hilarious at the time but knowing my friend well, I am aware that he hates thinking he has made any mistakes and is a master of covering them up with clever rhetoric. Perhaps it is worth noting that he was once a politician.

Why do we do this? What is it that terrifies us so much that we don't want to be seen to have made a mistake?

Politics

Making mistakes in politics is seen as the worst possible thing any politician can do. If, for example, the Prime Minister makes a U-turn on a certain policy it is seen as a weakness and not only that, it can undermine the confidence people have in the Government.

Why? Surely it is far better that they get the policy right? Surely it shows great wisdom and strength to admit a mistake and head off in a better direction?

We realise of course that it is because making a U-turn apparently tells the voters that a mistake has been made and thus the PM is not fit for his[1] job. Thus it is better for him to keep driving forward with the same policy despite recognising its folly, using all the rhetorical tricks possible to convince everyone that the decision they made in the first place, with a few minor corrections, was always the correct one. Margaret Thatcher is well known for her insistence on pursuing her policies, even if the facts clearly showed the wisdom of a different approach.

Haven't we got our sensibilities and priorities all wrong here?

The conundrum is that we would actually prefer that they made the right decisions, yet we are so programmed through historical perceptions of politics and constant 'feeding' by the media that we also see the whole process of a 'U' turn as failure. Complicated, aren't we? Worse than that, as a result of our continuing perception, we actually encourage them to perpetuate this ridiculous process.

During the Second World War, Churchill formed a coalition government, which was in effect the perfect government of national unity as it contained the most talented and energetic people available to him, regardless of party. He realised that to ensure the very best government and defence for the nation, a coalition was by far the best and most sensible choice. When all were responsible for the future of Britain, the parties worked together for the survival of their nation. This process was effective and was much more representative of the nation's political landscape than the 'first past the post' system. Why then did we change it back to the current system, which tends to move in a zigzag motion as Governments rise and fall?

Children are great at making mistakes

Young children on the other hand constantly make mistakes. They just get on with what they are doing and simply respond to what happens. If they have made a mistake they certainly don't worry about it. They either fix it, make it work or just move on to do something else. It never occurs to them that there is anything wrong with making a mistake. Why? Is it because they don't recognise it as a mistake in the first place? Is it that it is us, the 'sane and sensible' adults living in a world of duality (which young children haven't recognised yet) where things are good or bad, wrong or right and everything we do (and of course what everyone else does) we rate on a scale of success or failure?

When I watched my children drawing as youngsters I was always amazed and delighted at the simplicity, strength and speed with which they drew. They did not spend their time concerning themselves whether they could draw or not or whether the object looked exactly like it should – they just drew it. I recall a wonderful drawing my son Ted (aged about 6) presented to me. At the bottom of the page was a long sausage-like shape with one end rounded and the other end pointed. It was green. At the top of the page were two zigzag lines across the page, drawn with paint.

'This is great Ted', I said. 'Tell me about it'.

He looked at me quizzically. 'Can't you see? It's a crocodile!'

Suddenly I could see the crocodile in the sausage-like object at the bottom, so we discussed crocs for a moment. We had recently seen some on a trip to Zimbabwe.

'So what is this up here?' I asked, pointing at the zigzag lines. He turned and looked at me aghast. 'Can't you see? Those are its teeth. They have really big nasty sharp teeth!'

I sat back, delighted by what I was looking at. It was as if a veil had suddenly lifted from before my eyes. It was beautiful; stunning, in fact. For him it was the perfect way to draw a crocodile. The teeth, the most frightening part did not need to be in the crocodile's mouth to illustrate the point of how big and frightening they were, and in fact could not have been expressed in a better way. If he were to have drawn the crocodile several years later, he would most likely have felt compelled to put the teeth back in its mouth in order to make it look 'right'. What is this 'right' way, and what causes us to start drawing or doing things the 'right' way?

Ted has always drawn beautifully but it took one comment from an inconsiderate art teacher to stop him in his tracks and although he now draws occasionally, he has determined for himself that drawing is not his strong point. How could one comment have had such an impact on him and sustained itself so rigorously?

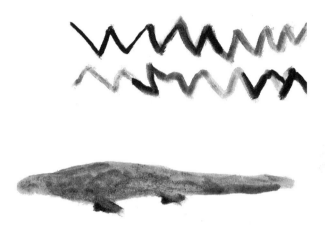

Ted's crocodile

The two inspired quotes

Let's go back to the two quotes that came to me as I sat in the class waiting for the negotiation to start.

"When I reach the next world, they will not ask me why I was not Moses. They will ask me why I was not Zuzya".

What is Rabbi Zuzya saying? It is reminding us that perhaps our primary mission in life is not to copy and emulate someone else, not to achieve great things, not to make a fortune, not to create a great community and produce a wonderful family (important and as wonderful as these things are) but rather to find out who we really are. To be ourselves and not only that, to become our own best friends; in fact I would go one step further – to actually fall in love with ourselves. How many of us can honestly say we have achieved that?

'*Love thy neighbour as thyself*' is one of Christ's most well-known and important teachings. I have always understood it to mean that I should be thoughtful and generous to those around me and to consider others less fortunate than myself. It was Charles Handy, author and philosopher who made me think again. He helped me notice the last two words in the statement. '*..as thyself*'. Suddenly I could see what Christ meant and it was much more than I had come to understand. If I loved my neighbour as I loved myself, then I realised he was getting a pretty shoddy deal and unless I truly loved myself, then I would never be able to love my neighbour adequately. So the question becomes, how do I love myself? Clearly it is not an egoical love; it has to be something completely different.

I have devoted a whole chapter to this (chapter 6) but the point to note here is that the more 'at one' we feel with ourselves, the less our egos drive our actions. Our egos are essentially brilliant survival mechanisms and help us to find a path through the challenges of daily life but they are not us. Our egos are extremely hungry and feed off all the inputs coming at us on a daily basis. Whether the information is good or bad, our egos munch at it – it is literally the foodstuff, the energy the ego needs to survive. It does not matter whether you are the 'egomaniac' at school who seems to have everything going his way, or the 'timid' one at the back of the class who tries to blend into the background, it is the ego that primarily drives our actions. It chomps away at all the information, good or bad. If good, then it rejoices. If bad then it causes us to writhe in agony but it gobbles it up just the same.

The ego only survives in a position of such extraordinary power because we give it permission to do so. We have allowed it full reign and it partakes in every conversation we have, every movie we watch, every book we read and every relationship we have. In fact, it is often at its most obvious in relationships with family and loved ones.

Inherent in all of us is a desire to feel good. Feeling bad is uncomfortable and so we will do pretty much anything to feel good. Amongst the many things this desire encourages us to do is to 'fit in', to be a 'part of the crowd'. Just being 'accepted' is often a great relief. We feel validated. What we don't want is to stand out from the crowd in a negative way, to be seen as the odd one out or the one who dressed inappropriately, or the one that asks the stupid question. Our survival mechanism will do everything it can to block such situations from occurring.

What becomes obvious is that we don't like to feel as if we have done something that might disrupt our fragile position, so we prefer not to make mistakes and certainly not publically (or privately for that matter, as we generally become our own fiercest critics). We are afraid. Most would deny this, but all of this is driven by fear. This fear is encouraged by our dependence on external verification and validation and in the process of seeking and needing this validation, we forget who we really are.

So how can we change this?

There is a quiet voice that is constantly talking to us – our intuition. Located in the same place from whence it comes is our heart. The heart is our core centre, part of the intuitive self and separate from the ego. It has no investment in proving anything to anyone. It sees life as a great adventure. It does not mind if we make mistakes; indeed it sees them as a way to gain greater understanding and unencumbered by the ego, allows us to see the funny side of our errors. Our challenge is to listen to this voice. Jiddu Krishnamurti (the Indian philosopher) once said that we should listen, not to what others say, but to what is actually taking place in ourselves. If we can do this without fear or arrogance, then we are touching on who we really are; that is the part of us to which Rabbi Zuzya refers.

Broken glass

"I never realised that broken glass could shine so brightly."

The second quote is a great reminder that whatever it is that we might do wrong serves as experience and it helps to build up a broader picture of how to handle life. What may look broken, embarrassing and agonisingly awful might, if we give it the chance, become the perfect lesson we need on our journey and indeed might actually be part of or stimulate a solution.

I have several friends who fit into a category that I would describe as 'having wisdom'. They are gentle but effective, they carry no airs or graces and they love life. They have great humour and laugh at themselves often.

Amongst all of them, one aspect of their nature stands out; they do not need to justify themselves. They have no egoical investment in being or needing to be 'right'. Nor do they see mistakes as mistakes. They see them as part of the learning process and thus 'mistakes' are laughed at and with great humour they move on. They recognise that in every learning process errors will be made. It is a necessary part of our personal development as out of these so called 'mistakes' come new and inventive ideas which help us all to move on (provided we allow them to formulate, rather than spending that possibly creative time beating ourselves up for getting it wrong in the first place).

Perhaps the best way to grasp this is to stand on one leg with one bare foot on the ground and the other foot balanced against the opposite knee. As you stand there, the standing leg and foot will constantly make adjustments to maintain balance. It suggests that the body hasn't worked it out and is over-correcting the whole time, making one error after another. The body is constantly learning and will eventually begin to make the correct adjustments and the 'wobble' will slow down considerably.

So it is with life. We are constantly making errors and we should expect to. The trick is to recognise that the 'wobble' is a necessary part of finding the answer, so appreciate it rather than despise it.

Morihei Ueshiba, the founder of Aikido was asked by a student (after watching him spar with an accomplished fighter) "You never seem to lose your balance. What is your secret?"

"You are wrong," Ueshiba replied. "I am constantly losing my balance. My skill lies in my ability to regain it."[2]

I recently participated in a discussion between mediators where the subject being discussed was anger and whether it may be a necessary part of the healing process. Naturally anger can get out of hand if not managed sensibly leading to all manner of very unpleasant happenings. For most of us, allowing ourselves to get angry is seen as a mistake, a loss of control but sometimes it is creative and healing. Sometimes it is good to vent one's frustration and anguish as it helps to release a pressure that we ourselves have allowed to build up over a period of time. The release of this energy, plus the fact that what needed to be said has been said can often free us up to move forward.

Life is an adventure

Imagine yourself on an adventure holiday where challenges constantly come up that need to be solved. Sometimes they are small, sometimes really quite taxing and you need to think your way through them. Sometimes the solutions work, sometimes they don't but it doesn't stop you from coming up with another possible solution. In this scenario we don't question it as we are expecting the challenges to occur, and neither do we see them as 'mistakes' – just possible solutions. When children are exploring new places, new ideas and new toys, this is exactly the approach they take.

Is this not a more natural and obvious approach to life? After all, through sheer experience, we know that not all of our initial solutions will work all of the time. That is all part of our learning process.

Sir Ken Robinson, a leading educational authority, noted in a recent talk that unless we are prepared and willing to make mistakes then we will never come up with anything original. He is right. We need to look at being 'wrong' in an entirely different way and see the 'wobble' as part of life's great adventure. View it with humour and relish the chance to try things out. If we do that, we are on the way to allowing ourselves to be original thinkers: a chance to really stand firmly on the ground – one 'wobble' at a time!

¹ *I generically refer to both male and female Prime Ministers.*

² *Morihei Ueshiba (1883 –1969) was a famous martial artist and founder of the Japanese martial art of Aikido. He is often referred to as 'the founder' Kaiso or Ōsensei, 'Great Teacher'.*

8

Are you willing to embrace change?

The key to remaining fresh and energised

"Standing water stagnates. Keep it moving and it becomes the elixir of life."

Some years ago our washing machine died on us. One of my sons was nine at the time and going through a stressful period at school. When the suppliers of the new washing machine arrived and started moving the old one out, he yelped and charged out of the room into the courtyard (where the workman had stopped for a breather) and threw himself over the washing machine, refusing them permission to take it anywhere. He was determined that it should not go and fought valiantly to hang onto it. Eventually we convinced him that the new one would look much the same as the other one when in place and that it would mean all the clothes would be washed and be nice and clean for school the next day.

He was very upset to see the old machine go and it took a while for us to recognise that as he was going through a stressful period, he needed one area of his life to remain stable and unchanged and that was home. We noticed it with other things. For example when he accidentally broke a bit of china, a replacement was not acceptable. Getting the piece repaired was the only way forward because then things seemed unchanged.

What he was experiencing was a fear that if the 'safe' world around him began to change then he would have no solid base, no rock on which he could brace his feet. Every young person goes through these agonies at various stages in their lives.

Adults too have moments when they need the safety of a solid base or an unchanging home, particularly if they are going through deeply stressful or depressing moments in their lives as it provides the stability they need in order to move on.

All this 'solidity' is external

I wonder if you have considered or noticed that so much of this 'solidity' we search for is external to us; it is beyond our human form and as a result is beyond our control. 'Of course', you might say, 'it has always been so and always will be'.

I beg to differ.

Children are by design dependant on us for a period of time. I wonder though, whether we encourage them to be more dependent on us as adults than they need to be? Is it partly because we want them to in some way to remain dependent on us for our own justification? Or is it simply a fear of letting go? We provide all sorts of boundaries around them which are quite right and necessary at first but we tend to leave the boundaries up for longer than perhaps is necessary and not only that, we give them little real guidance on how to start building their own internal boundaries and guidelines when they are ready to do so. We prefer to say 'keep following the boundaries we have set for you because we know they are right'.

The point here is that as long as we are dependent on external boundaries, on 'fitting in' with what our parents, schools or society says is the right thing to do, we remain limited in our ability to widen our own experiences.

Those amongst us who are most likely to succeed in whatever endeavour they have chosen are those who are not constricted by these boundaries, the 'norms' that they see around them. They are happy to fit in momentarily from a social point of view, but they are not firm members of the club. They can fit elsewhere with consummate ease. They have created their own internal boundaries and guidelines, quite separate from the external ones and are able to operate from within rather than from without.

I recall a speech day at a School attended by my sons some years ago where a well-known Conservative politician was giving a rousing speech on the importance of bringing our youngsters up to 'think for themselves', to be 'independent from the crowd' and to 'walk their own walk'. This was received with rapturous applause and many cries of 'Hear hear'. Later I was asked to join a group of parents for a picnic lunch where the speech was discussed with great approval. Someone said 'Thank goodness we all think independently and are capable of ploughing our own furrows'. At this point discussion moved on to other issues such as hunting, horses, shooting, fishing and politics, all subjects that could have created some exciting debate. It didn't, and I sat there wondering after 45 minutes or so where this 'independent furrow' was? I certainly couldn't see it. Who was kidding who I wondered?

It is easy to believe we are being independently minded and 'doing our own thing' when we are doing nothing more that fitting in with the 'norms' around us and running with the herd. Of course we are all independently minded to a point but the question is whether we are internally secure enough to step out and do something that is out of the 'norm' when the opportunity stares us in the face? Equally, those who follow the 'norm' are not usually happy with change unless it is 'good' or 'convenient' change.

Why are we so afraid of change?

Change can be very minor and not affect much at all, especially if we have created the change ourselves. That is easy to deal with. Change on the other hand can be very dramatic and can seriously affect our lives. These are the moments when we are less likely to be content with it. So what is it about change that we find so disarming?

It is the fact that it is uncontrollable and generally unpredictable. It just happens and there is really not much we can do about it. Change can come in the form of a flood, the car blowing up, political change or the start of a war and all of these can be seen as negative changes. But are they? Sometimes those changes that appear to be dreadful may well be the start of something much more rewarding. For example, someone made redundant one day may finally decide to get up and do something for themselves and write a book or set up a business or become a teacher or similar, so be careful not to judge change as either good or bad.

I recall a wonderful story of an old Chinaman which touches on exactly this point.

"There was once an old man in China who had a beautiful stallion much admired by all his neighbours. One day the stallion leaped out of the corral and disappeared. Everyone came round to see the old man to say how sorry they were for his terrible misfortune. "Misfortune?" said the old man, "What misfortune? How do you know it is misfortune?"
Two weeks later the stallion re-appeared, bringing with it 20 mares which it brought into the corral. Everyone came to congratulate him on his good fortune. "Good fortune?" he asked. "What good fortune? How do you know this is good fortune?"
10 days later, whilst breaking in one of the new mares, his son fell from the horse and broke one of his legs. The neighbours all came to say how sorry they were for his terrible misfortune.
A few weeks later, the men from the Government came and took all the able bodied young men to go to war, but they were unable to take the old man's son as his leg was broken. All the neighbours came round to see the old man to congratulate him on his extraordinary good fortune....and so the story goes on.[1]

The point of course is that we should not judge the changes in our lives. We should hold our judgement and rather than sitting and waiting to see what might come of them, embrace them and move with them.

Anchors

Another way of describing the 'solidity' we seek is to see it as a need for anchors. Many years ago I came home one day to find that the entrance hall had been re-configured and whilst everything looked very tidy, it was all in the 'wrong' place. After a short 'discussion', I shifted certain things back to where they were before. They were perhaps not so well organised in the old position, but I liked them that way and that is where they felt 'right'.

Why did I make such a fuss? Why didn't I just accept it as being a really good idea? There are many reasons why people react the way they do but in this case it is because, rather like my son and the washing machine, we have certain 'anchors'. If they are in the correct place and remain unchanged, then we are content.

Imagine for a moment thousands of imaginary ropes that run from you to all sorts of things in your life that cause you to feel comfortable. This does not just include material possessions but everything about you: for example your family history, your parents, colour, race, religion, culture, nationality, economic status and politics. It could be the way your bedroom is laid out, the place where you park the car each day, cooking supper for your children each night and of course the opinions of others (often the most pernicious of them all). We easily become dependent upon them to keep us 'steady' and 'balanced'. They give us a sense of place – an identity.

The challenge is that all of these anchors are external of us (apart from our genetic history) and are therefore liable to change. The more dependent we are on external anchors, the more affected we will be by the changes that happen around us, since our 'comfort' is found in the external.

Finding, or rather relaxing into our intuitive selves is central to having a strong internal anchor. When we recognise that we are already perfect just because we exist, we have finally reached the place of true solidity. After that, what happens to us externally may affect us but it no longer controls us: our true security comes from within. All the external anchors are still there but the ropes connecting us with them are no longer rigid. They are thinner, looser and extendable. It places us in a much stronger position to move forward seeing the benefits of change, rather than fearing it.

Imagine not being heavily affected by external events that would normally cause you to worry unnecessarily? Imagine being able to enjoy life and know that you can far better cope with any situation without resorting to panic? Imagine being able to go anywhere in the world at any time and feel comfortable, without needing to know there is a McDonalds or an Expatriate Club nearby to which you could anchor yourself? That would be true freedom.

The final words of the poem 'Invictus'[2] by William Ernest Henley remind us that we can be physically free with no external restrictions whatsoever and yet still be prisoners of our external anchors, or we can be confined in prison for 27 years (like Mandela) under the total physical control of others and yet be completely free, anchored within.

"It matters not how strait the gate,
How charged with punishments the scroll,
I am the master of my fate,
I am the captain of my soul."

Using intuitive drawing as a way to loosen the anchors

Some of the people who attend my intuitive drawing courses are already established artists who have found themselves in ruts and wish to find some way of breaking out. Others are from the business world with unfulfilling jobs who are searching for a way to unleash their creativity.

Why do we create ruts for ourselves? Is it because the anchors we have tied ourselves to keep us feeling so comfortable that we can't let go or are we too afraid to try something different?

When drawing intuitively, we are working from a completely different perspective and it allows for wonderfully creative ideas to flow from us without the constriction of our anchors. The key to intuitive drawing is that it is spontaneous and without considered thought. That way it remains free and flowing and what we are left with are examples of our own creative ability. It helps us to recognise how much easier it is to loosen the ties to our anchors than we believe it really is.

Try it for yourself. You may be surprised by your own creations.

[1] *I heard this story in a sermon many years ago and have never been able to trace its origins. I suspect it is part of Chinese folklore.*

[2] *'Invictus' by William Ernest Henley (1849–1903) is a well-known poem that was treasured by Nelson Mandela whilst imprisoned on Robben Island.*

Wire and leaves – intuitive drawing with found objects.

9

Do you honestly trust yourself?

"If a man does not keep pace with his companions, perhaps it is because he hears a different drummer. Let him step to the music which he hears, however measured and far away."
Henry David Thoreau – extract from 'Walden' (1817-1862)

My son Jasper attended a school CCF (Combined Cadet Force)[1] weekend during which they were split into orienteering groups and had to locate and mark different checkpoints using a map. After several hours of this he was beginning to get bored when suddenly he noticed that a number of small groups seemed to be converging on the same checkpoint at roughly the same time. To spark things up and have some fun, he yelled out "My God! Here come the enemy!" and started running full tilt down the path. As he ran, one by one all the groups started running in the same direction as he was. When he dashed into a small wood they all followed him in and found him sitting there roaring with laughter. "Why have you followed me," he asked. "Who is the enemy?"

Recounting this story to me later with much laughter, he said how amazed he was that everyone just followed him blindly, that 'herd mentality' seemed to grip them all and they felt they needed to follow. It surprised him that people could be so easily persuaded to act without reason, especially when he was talking nonsense in the first place. There was no enemy and they knew it, so who were they running from?

In Chapter 5, I allude to the ease with which we follow rules and instructions handed out by others, often without any sensible reason at all. I remember many years ago I entered a hotel and there was a man standing in the lounge area speaking to a group of people. As I walked past, he turned to me and said "Here. Hold this". He handed me a tray of empty glasses. I stood there holding the tray wondering what to do next. He kept talking. So after a minute or so I said "excuse me, what do you want me to do with this?"

He looked at me with a rather questioning look on his face. "Why are you asking me?"

"You just gave it to me" I said.

"You took it!" he said. "What you do with it is no concern of mine". Everyone roared with laughter and I was left standing there feeling a complete idiot holding a tray of empty glasses in front of a group of people I did not know.

I learnt a lot from this experience. Let's look at the lessons in order as we then begin to see a flow of learning taking place. Initially I was more concerned with my actions and my feelings:

1) At first it was the pain and the shame I felt at being so stupid. I couldn't believe I could have been so dumb as to take the tray and to stand there for ages holding it, especially full of empty glasses, in the middle of a hotel foyer!

2) I asked myself why I took the tray. Was it good manners? I convinced myself it must have been. I had done the right thing in the circumstances. Anyone would have done it. (Here I was trying to comfort myself).

3) Why did I hold it for so long? Why did I feel I had to ask him what I should do with them? After all, it was just a bunch of dirty glasses. I figured that I must be a complete idiot to have done what I did. I wondered what was wrong with me. Why hadn't I just laughed it off? Of course I had laughed with them in the foyer, but underneath it all I was in agony.

After that I tried really hard to forget it but it kept nudging back into my mind at different points in my life, with none other than my intuition doing the nudging. It was bringing me back to the moment, saying effectively 'revisit this: there is more to learn'. So I began a new learning process. I started to look at it from a different perspective.

1) I was at that time in my life pretending to be more confident than I actually was and spent a lot of time trying to draw attention to myself as one of the lads. As a result, anything that 'ruffled' the illusion I was trying to create was a punch in the ribs, reminding me that I wasn't as 'cool' as I was pretending to be.

2) Because I was so dependent on the opinion of others around me, I hated making mistakes as I felt they would damage my 'standing'. On the other hand, if I was revered for doing something 'cool', then I was elated. I was fixated on the 'illusion' of myself I was projecting outwards and thus on the external rather than the real me that was internal. My state of mind moved in a zigzag of highs and lows as a result.

3) I so easily accepted a most unusual instruction from someone I didn't know. The man had not asked me to hold the tray; he had instructed me to hold it. As a result I didn't question it. Why didn't I stop and think about it before acting? It wasn't as if it was an emergency or anything. What was it that caused me to do what my son Jasper's friends did and just blindly follow the instruction given?

I have of course already covered some of this in my earlier chapters where I discuss the 'filter' and all the many different experiences we have in our lives that affect the opinion we have of ourselves. We receive an awfully large amount of conditioning as we grow up, particularly at school and in other organisations that demand action on command and have very strict rules. It is easy to get buoyed into a mentality that simply responds to orders without thinking too much about them. This is certainly part of the reason but it is definitely not the full picture.

A Lack of Trust

The all-encompassing reason though is that I did not trust myself and my own judgement. I was still looking externally for reassurance. Trust is a difficult concept to grasp at the best of times but perhaps it can best be described in this short anecdote. If I want to learn to ride a bicycle, I have to trust that I will eventually get it right. Usually we learn when we are still children and the 'comfort trust' comes from our parents. 'Go on darling, you can do it! We believe in you. On you go'. It is their reassurance and trust in our ability that buoys us up and gives us the confidence to take the next step.

As we grow up, so our own internal compass takes over (or should) and to a greater or lesser degree, we begin to trust ourselves. If, like I was, you are very dependent on the external opinion, then you will practice where no-one can see you and make sure you get it right first so you look 'cool' when others can see you. Why?

I suggest that the thought of 'messing up' in front of others would severely damage the image we have of ourselves and that we are attempting to portray. Of course, if one is naturally good at sport and well balanced and enjoy a certain 'credibility' as a result of that, one may 'play to the crowd' and 'show off' how easy it is to learn to ride the bike. Both are ego driven approaches. If we are all learning to ride together, we take comfort in the fact that others are going through the same challenges that we are.

Millions of people across the world trust in God. Religions of course encourage us to trust and have faith in God. Here we are accepting on faith their explanations to us that God is there and will protect us. Many would say they have real experience of God's love for us and therefore their trust in God is based on their own personal experience. For most though it is a blind trust but one that brings extraordinary comfort to so many right across the world.

Blind trust however can end in calamity. During the 2nd world war, millions of Jews put their trust in God and many did not move from where they were living (particularly in Austria) when they knew the Nazis were coming, trusting that God would protect them. Instead they were horded together and transported to Auschwitz and other camps where many of them later died. Most of those who did move (often to the disgust of those who did not, as they considered this to be an extreme lack of trust in God) survived, whether in other European Countries, the USA or in Palestine.

How do we trust ourselves?

In all of the above examples we are looking at having trust in something external to us which in turn gives us an 'anchor' around which we can cast our rope. It is easier to trust others than it is to trust ourselves. Putting our faith in God and God's laws for example may help to keep us on the straight and narrow, but as long as they remain external guidelines/rules from an external source without our having cemented them in as our own personal rules/guidelines, we remain at the mercy of our own ego and of course of others. For example, I may be a regular churchgoer who believes fervently in Christ's teaching 'Love thy neighbour as thyself', but find I have bitter and vengeful thoughts towards certain others who were perhaps cruel to me or others in the past. In Christian terms, these would be considered 'sinful' thoughts and because of that I feel a constant sense of guilt. So now I need to plead for forgiveness for my sins. Then the feelings return, I feel guilty once more and this never-ending cycle begins afresh.

I am not so sure this is right.

If I am continuously feeling guilty and worried that I have 'sinned' yet again, how can I ever develop any real trust in myself? I would hold a perpetual feeling of unworthiness. Certainly I can't change the experiences I have had in the past, but I can step aside from them and look at them from a 'helicopter' viewpoint, seeing them in the wider context. For example, feeling vengeful thoughts towards someone may not be a Christian value but given my experiences from the past, they are perfectly understandable as they fit with the egoical responses to such incidents. The choice I have therefore is whether to feel it is sinful to think them, or whether I recognise it is a natural response which I can choose to ignore. If I see it from the perspective of my intuitive self it might give me a completely different answer. The answer might be, 'does it really matter anymore?'

So how do we begin?

The first stage is to face life honestly. Don't hide from issues that need dealing with. Have the courage to deal with these rather than avoid them. Instead of worrying about them and fearing the possible outcomes, see them as part of the solution, whatever the outcome.

The second stage is in recognising that we are not what the 'filter' suggests we are (see chapter 6). We are more than that, and the way we discover it is to relax into ourselves, slow down and remind ourselves of our childhood approach to life. Children, at an early stage, just 'are'. They are wonderfully authentic. They are not concerned with whether they are good or bad at something, how they look, whether they are fat or thin, they just get on with it. If it doesn't work, they move on. Their approaches are often described as simplistic but equally, some of our greatest sages, after years of contemplation have returned to that simplistic position and indeed often advise that we should also. Children have a delightfully naïve sense of confidence in whatever they do. A child is able to receive openly; there is no judgment, they take life as it is. They feel abundant with whatever they have, whether it is a cooking pot or a very expensive toy. It is only later that we 'learn' to judge ourselves against others. What if, rather than judging ourselves, we consciously reminded ourselves of how abundant we are already, starting with our existence, our health, our family and friends and the ability to think and to feel joy?

As explained earlier, we keep searching for 'anchors', whether they are religious beliefs, cultural perceptions, ideologies, the pronouncements of people we respect or even myths. We hang on to them because they reassure us during uncertain times, often believing that they are 'truths'. These 'truths' give us comfort and make us feel more secure. They are however all external.

In stepping back from the ego and the external 'rules' and perceptions and slowly relaxing into ourselves, we connect with the intuitive self. We need to trust that we don't require all the 'structures' and 'supports' in the filter or the external 'rules' and that we will slowly be revealed to ourselves. This is where the heart is, the relaxed, spontaneous, easy-going, non-judgemental, truly authentic person which exists in all of us and in whom we can place our trust.

Having the courage to step out of line

All of us have developed confidence in certain areas along the way but these confidences are subject to fluctuation, dependent on our reliance on external opinion and of course our changing abilities.

Imagine for a moment what it would be like to be free from the need for physical and psychological certainty all the time? Imagine being able to feel your own internal security so strongly that you felt secure even in the midst of a time of great turbulence? Would that not be true mental liberation? Would it not allow you the complete freedom to do and be whatever it is you believed in without feeling constrained by ideological, social or financial constraints - to just be, with grace and ease?

When people have an approach to life that everything is an adventure it takes the sting out of 'failure'. Think like a child again and have a go. If it doesn't work, take several deep breaths to ease away from the 'egoical' self, pick up the pieces and try again. Make it a core rule not to spend time re-running the egoical responses to failure as this only causes pain and debilitation. After all, there may be wisdom in your apparent 'failure' which could provide you with the key to move forward with your plans.

Trusting in your ability to achieve something different and original requires courage but if it is based squarely on your own values, rules and abilities, you will find it a whole lot easier to accomplish. It requires stepping up to the line and taking a bold step into the unknown. It may be a new idea you are presenting to your boss. It maybe something completely different you have always wanted to do. Whatever it is, feel into whatever it is you want to achieve. Ask yourself why it is so important you. This is vital as you might well find that those whom you love around you don't want you to change and will do everything in their power to stop you, telling you that it is in your own and their best interests not to do so. Most people are afraid of change.

When you really start focusing on what you wish to achieve, you create an energy around you which itself starts searching for opportunities. You will begin to meet people or read things that impact directly on what you are trying to do and your intuition will have a field day throwing up all sorts of ideas for you to consider.

One of the best descriptions of this phenomenon is described by W.H. Murray[2]. He describes it as 'providence'.

"Until one is committed, there is hesitancy, the chance to draw back, always ineffectiveness.
Concerning all acts of initiative (and creation), there is one elementary truth, the ignorance of which kills countless ideas and splendid plans: that the moment one definitely commits oneself, then providence moves too.
All sorts of things occur to help one that would never otherwise have occurred. A whole stream of events issue from the decision, raising in one's favour all manner of unforeseen incidents and meetings and material assistance, which no man could have dreamed would come his way."

W.H. Murray (1913–1996) The Scottish Himalayan Expedition, JM Dent,1951

Trusting that progress will happen rather than worrying that it will not

I recall many years ago my brother Sim and I were speaking about the issue of money and in mid conversation he said to me "I think about money all the time".

"So do I." I said.

"That's true", he said. "The difference is that I think about how much money I am going to make and what I will do with it, whilst you think about how much money you haven't got."

This was a profound learning point for me and it was quite correct. If you dwell on what you can't do, or how much money you haven't got, guess what? You continue to have no money. The very process of worrying about what money you don't have causes you to think of how little you can do about it. On the other hand, if you consider what you could do, the more your intuition and mind start the process of finding ways to achieve this.

By trusting that you will achieve what you want and effectively 'releasing' it from the bondage of fear and worry, you will surprise yourself with your ability to intuitively come up with creative ideas. This fits exactly with W.H. Murray's statement above. He does not speak about worrying – he speaks of moving forward, feeling into it and trusting that the process will work. Creativity is problem solving by definition.

Literally creating our own future

Trusting that you can make it happen is crucial but there is an additional aspect to all this which really does work and may seem rather surprising. If you genuinely trust that something will occur and you can clearly see it in your mind's eye and can feel what it will be like once it is happening, then you literally imagine it into existence. By this I don't mean a whimsical dream which pops into your head from time to time. What I mean is that when you determine there is something you wish to achieve, when you trust that it will happen and that you can see it, smell it and feel it as if it is already in existence, then it has no alternative but to evolve. As W.H. Murray points out in the quote above, 'providence moves too'.

The key to allowing this is in capturing the feeling of it already being done. Does it make you feel joy? It should do! It automatically lifts your energy to a higher vibration. Keeping that vibration high is critical to providing the scenario for these things to be attracted into your life. It is a bit like living in two worlds at the same time. The real world and the world you have created in your imagination, where you feel so much better. Visionaries have always lived there, which is why they have been so effective at attracting things into their lives.

This may seem totally unrealistic and yet it is exactly what happens to each of us every day. We are in the lifestyle we lead right now because we simply don't see ourselves living any other way. When we think forwards (which is effectively creating an imaginary world since it has not yet materialised), we generally perceive the future as being remarkably similar to our recent past i.e. bills to pay, dogs to feed, jobs to complete and car servicing to be done and paid for. None of these are wrong but if they are the only way we see our lives progressing, then nothing ever changes. It becomes a closed loop of self-justifying results.

Those who are wealthy generally maintain their wealth as they see and feel themselves living within that environment. Those who are poor continuously live from hand to mouth because they simply can't see themselves living any other way. Yet there are those born into wealth that go broke and stay that way and those who come from extremely poor backgrounds who are now exceptionally wealthy. How does this happen? Is it luck or bad luck, or could it be that they literally imagined their lifestyles into being?

Of course it could be argued that it has to do with the realities of life and there are genuine reasons why the poor are always poor and the rich stay rich. These arguments may well be absolutely correct and yet despite this, they only give a limited part of the picture. Note these examples.

I have a retired friend who lives not far from us. She has a small semi-detached house and a tiny car and a monthly budget which she never sticks to. She always goes over budget enjoying her life, knowing that funds will come from somewhere to cover the bills, and they always do. Whether it is a gift, a legacy, some temporary work or a windfall, somehow it always works out. She simply trusts that the money will come and it does.

This is where most of us would go wrong as we would wonder where the money might come from. We would try to reason a specific sequence of events which would lead to the money coming in and in the process we would limit our potentials. Trusting that it will happen and keeping our options very much open as to how it will happen is critical to the success of such a process.

I am not advocating that everyone should suddenly start living beyond their means and hope for the best. What I am suggesting is that we consider her mind-set. What is it about the way she thinks, feels, senses and acts that is different to ours and allows her to live this way?

Recently a young man named Jake Bugg hit the music scene here in the UK and has become a very popular young singer. Less than a year ago he was living with his mother who was on income support. He apparently had only one pair of trousers and one pair of shoes to his name. In a recent press interview[3], he said that he used to imagine in such detail what he would be doing when he became successful that when it happened, the lifestyle seemed completely normal. He slipped into it with such surprising ease because he had lived it in his mind already. He trusted that it would happen and so it was just a matter of time before it became a reality.

I suggest that once he was sure about what he wished to achieve and indeed believed it possible, his intuition led him to make the right decisions that paved the way to his success.

Again, it could be argued that he is a very talented musician and songwriter and so was destined for success anyway but there are many others out there who are also equally talented, perhaps even more so. Why don't they find themselves in his position?

For some, progress can happen quite quickly. For others, change happens in small incremental steps, rather like watching a building being built. Impatience can destroy genuine progress so it is really important not to overlook small steps. Trust, have patience and be grateful for all the changes that do occur, even if they may appear negative to start with.

Allowing ourselves permission to do so: changing core beliefs

For some there is one area of restraint which does need consideration and that is our own refusal to let change happen. We may not like the way we live and long to be in better circumstances or indeed be very talented in some way but somehow we strangely find 'comfort' in being where we are, with anchors to which we are tightly tied. Thus it is not enough to just imagine a different lifestyle or even live it temporarily (for example, three out of every five professional footballers go broke within five years of retiring and similar figures exist for lottery winners). It might, for example, suit our political attitudes or our habit of blaming everyone else for our problems and perhaps it also keeps us within a certain social circle within which we are comfortable. Loosening ties to anchors is critical to being able to move on.

It might be that some of you have been brought up with core beliefs which are restricting your progress. For example you may have, ingrained in your filter, a solid belief that 'life will always be a struggle' or 'I will always be poor'. If that is deeply ingrained, then that is the message you are sending out and of course is what comes back to you as life responds by giving you what you expect.

Your everyday reality is a good indicator of your core beliefs. For example, what does your reality look like? Is it happy, loving, joyful and prosperous or full of blame, hate, anger and violence? Are you your own fiercest critic? Think what that criticism is based on (in other words, what standards are you trying to live by which are causing you to be so critical of yourself) and it will give you an indication of some of your key core beliefs. Many people fill their minds with what they fear and dread along with anger at themselves or others, rather than thoughts aligned more with their aspirations. This can all be changed but the first task is to work out what your core beliefs are; only with that knowledge will you be in a position to change them and thus begin the process of adjusting your reality.

You may need to consciously revoke some of your past beliefs (after all they have hung around for a long time and have had a profound effect on you up until now) and this can be done once you are clear as to what they are. Some of your core beliefs may even be the stimulus for some of your darkest fears, so it is quite important to recognise what they are so that they can be changed.

Another important point is that some of us are really bad at receiving, whether a compliment, a gift or a comfortable lifestyle. We feel we don't deserve it. Why not? What have we done that condemns us to thinking this way? Why is it OK for others but not us? Where did these core beliefs come from and why? From our parents, our religion, our culture?

As a consequence and in particular it is really important that we detach ourselves from our parents' values and beliefs as for the majority of us they are inherited and they form the basis of our own. It is only by freeing ourselves from them that we can decide what beliefs we wish to follow by our own choice and for our own journey. We may decide to continue to follow all or some of their core values and beliefs but it must be by our choice, not theirs (which it always is in our formative years). Some of their beliefs may be wise, clear cut and sensible whilst others may be out-dated, crippling and based on their own egoical weaknesses.

We therefore all need to give ourselves permission to think differently, to ask ourselves these challenging questions and to release any need to fulfil certain beliefs that have been handed on to us. This is our journey and ours alone. If our core beliefs are not in order then we are making life extremely difficult for ourselves. It is like plodding through a muddy field when we could be walking comfortably along the path nearby.

Andy Murray's pep-talk

In a recent press interview[4], British tennis player Andy Murray spoke about how his life turned around in a deep conversation he had with himself in the lavatory during a break in the final of the US Open. It was September 12th 2012, the score was two sets all (he had been two sets up and had squandered the lead) and Murray felt dejected. His shoulders were hunched and his head hung low. He had spent the last 5 years being asked whether he would ever win a grand slam and he had begun to believe that perhaps they were right to doubt him. He had played in four grand slam finals and lost them all. As he looked at himself in the mirror with all these doubts whirling around his head, he realised he had to do something or else he would lose again. So he gave himself a pep-talk. He gazed into his own eyes and told himself loudly, over and over again that he could and would win the game. He says he felt something change inside himself and in that instant, he knew he could win.

What Murray had done was to allow a belief that he could not win a grand slam to establish itself firmly in his mind. It had become a core belief and was governing his progress. Once he recognised its presence, he realised he had to change it and in that pep-talk in front of the mirror, he reprogrammed that belief. The effect was immediate; he physically felt the change inside him and then went out and won the match. As he said himself, it was the moment his life turned around.

Recognising that we are the creators of our own lives is a mammoth step forward. The next step is to own it, grasp it and drink it in. Take several deep breaths and feel into these words: 'I made it and I can change it'.

Releasing the expectations of outcome – allowing for a flexible conclusion

This may seem completely illogical as every management guide and self-help book will tell you that it is critical to have a goal and a very clear goal as it gets work done. For example, if my goal is to clean all the windows, weed two flower beds and cook supper today, it is a good thing that it is clear. It gets done.

What I mean is that, when taking an idea from fruition to completion there may well be many changes along the way and necessary changes at that. If we are stuck with one goal in mind it may limit the outcome dramatically. There needs to be an openness to change. What we see in front of us are essentially 'potentials', possibilities of what might and could happen. They are aspirations. If we solidify these into very specific goals, then we lock in the final outcome which may not be nearly as creative, important or as useful as they might have become if we had allowed them to grow and perhaps even transmute into something else. So whilst we have a new creation (the original goal), it is perhaps a shadow of what it could have become had we not locked into the outcome.

Becoming overly tied to very specific goals limits our creativity. Creativity builds on itself all the time and our first idea may well evolve into something completely different and much more effective than perhaps the first idea may have been. I recall at Art College, as I approached my sculpture degree show (with 6 months to go), my course leader came and asked what I was planning. I had planned out exactly what I was going to make and how I was going to make it, with drawings to accompany my plans. They evolved as I had imagined they would and thus I was shocked to find I did not get a first class degree. 'Why not,' I asked?

'In the last six months you have not been creative' I was told. 'You have simply followed a blueprint. You have made what you intended, but in the process you have killed your creativity. You did not allow this work to evolve naturally. You pre-planned it and as a result the pieces are not nearly as powerful as they are likely to have been if you had allowed your creativity full reign. They might even have changed completely.'

My 'goal' was so clear that it stopped the process of creativity. That is a very powerful message for us all and requires some reflection. Equally, changing from a 'goal oriented' system into one in which we release the expectations of outcome requires going against the grain and that requires vision and courage.

The key point here and the reason I have spent so much time on it is that in trusting yourself, trusting in providence and being willing to embrace change and challenge the 'norm', you will be giving yourself the freedom to cultivate and develop original thoughts and allow them to evolve as they should, unrestricted by convention. That is creativity unleashed and we need that now more than ever as we emerge into a new and changing existence.

I have a wonderful book which is a compilation of the journals of a young man called Dan Eldon[5] who died at the age of 22 having completed in that short life what most people only accomplish in 80. He had travelled four continents, led expeditions across Africa, written a book, worked as a graphic designer in New York, made a film and had become a respected photojournalist for Reuters - all before he died tragically in Somalia in 1993. What Dan exhibited was this sense of adventure that I speak of, a willingness to step out and do something different because it meant something to him.

On one of the pages of the journals he writes "What is the difference between exploring and being lost? The Journey is the destination". The question he poses is a good one. Does it matter? If everything is a great adventure, surely it becomes irrelevant?

His last sentence became the title of the book and the message it offers is very clear. Having a single goal is very limiting. The journey of getting there (with all its ups, downs and changes) and beyond, is really the destination. Imagine it, trust it, feel it and then live it with joy and zest. That way it has no alternative but to manifest.

[1] The Combined Cadet Force (CCF) is a Ministry of Defence sponsored youth organisation in the United Kingdom. Its aim is to "provide a disciplined organisation in a school so that pupils may develop powers of leadership by means of training to promote the qualities of responsibility, self reliance, resourcefulness, endurance and perseverance".

[2] W.H. Murray (1913 –1996) was a Scottish mountaineer and writer, one of a group of active mountain climbers, before and just after World War II. The quote appears in 'The Scottish Himalayan Expedition', published by JM Dent (part of the Orion Group), 1951. All attempts to find the copyright holder were unsuccessful.

[3] The Times Weekend Review, February 16th 2013, Pop. 'I had one pair of jeans and no cash', by Ben Machell.

[4] The Times Magazine, March 30th 2013. 'Andy Murray uncovered' by Matthew Syed.

[5] 'The Journey is the Destination - The journals of Dan Eldon' was put together and edited by his mother, Kathy Eldon. He remains today an extraordinary example to others. Published by Booth Clibborn Editions. The Dan Eldon Foundation website can be found at www.daneldon.org

James Maberly

Intuitive drawing to the sound of different types of music by Tony King

10

What is the tone of your communication with others?

"I was angry with my friend:
I told my wrath, my wrath did end.
I was angry with my foe:
I told it not, my wrath did grow."

Excerpt from 'A Poison Tree' by William Blake (1757-1827)[1]

Being able to communicate effectively is one of the key abilities required for success in most ventures or activities in life. How we come over to others will determine their immediate response to us and indeed their future relationships with us. There is often a fine line between understanding and misunderstanding and a simple misperception can cause untold damage to relationships between friends, family, colleagues, communities and/or nations.

We live in a world where for thousands of years, conflicts between countries, races, tribes, religious and political groups have been regular and seemingly unavoidable. Millions upon millions of people have either died or had their livelihoods destroyed in the process. It has become a way of life, albeit one that very few of us relish.

Why on earth do we do this to each other? What is it in our psychological make-up that encourages us to perpetuate this continuous cycle of conflict and violence and (in some countries) the largest slice of budget being allocated to funding the military?

Of course we need to have in place a reasonable defence network to stand up against an aggressor, but at what point is that defence 'enough'?

Why can't we talk to one another?

Conflict and dispute are very ego-based. They exist in almost every area of life, whether the battlefield or the kitchen. What if, rather than having to resort to conflict or to the courts, we chose dialogue as a way to find a solution? Is this not what happened in Northern Ireland and in South Africa?

Obviously we cannot be naïve. There are some disputes where the very concept of dialogue seems so far away that solutions seem impossible. Yet, ultimately, even given the time it might take, dialogue has to be the way forward in resolving conflict. It is only through dialogue and consensus that parties can agree to move forward with a common aim in mind.

As a trained negotiator and mediator and especially whilst teaching negotiation skills[2], I have watched how people from different cultures can misinterpret each other remarkably easily and how simple it is to create misunderstandings which in turn grow into substantial issues of disagreement. I have seen that with a better understanding of how to communicate with one another, disputants have found ways of resolving issues much more easily.

The art of communication

The one person in my life who can trigger in me the most instant defensive reaction to a comment is my wife. She seems to have a button which hot-wires itself directly to my ego and I react, usually defensively and almost always incorrectly. She is my best friend but also the person I am most vulnerable to and as a result she is also one of my most important teachers. Every time I react it reminds me that I am responding from my ego, reacting as ever to a perceived threat. If I were to take a couple of deep breaths before I responded, it would all come out very differently. Not only would I actually 'hear' what she had just said but from the perspective of my intuitive self, I would see it in a different light.

We all have people in our lives who have access to our 'hot-wire buttons', some at home, some at work. Each of these people has their own hot-wire buttons and they each see things from their own particular perspective.

In negotiation training, we use a story about a woman who, in a desperate attempt to get across the river to be with her boyfriend, sleeps with the boat captain (his fee). Feeling guilty, she tells her boyfriend who instantly rejects her and throws her out. She tells a friend about it who, feeling sorry for her, immediately beats up her ex-boyfriend whilst she watches, laughing, in the background.

We ask the participants to grade who is the most honourable and downwards to the least honourable in the story. The responses are always at variance, particularly between men and women and where ideological and cultural differences exist, can be remarkably different. Heated arguments develop easily and have sometimes become quite intense reminding us all that, no matter who we are, we are each a bit like an iceberg. What shows on the surface is only a small portion of the whole picture. Having our own opinion is one thing but being tolerant of the views and ideologies of others is critical.

Being right and allowing others to be right

Indeed I would go one step further. Let us float upwards and take a 'helicopter' view of the different nations and religions across the world. For each of the people involved within these groups, certain truths abound. For them, whatever they believe is right is unquestionably right. After all, evidence presents itself to them regularly to justify their beliefs (anchors).

And so it is for us. We are no different. It also applies of course to anything we happen to be doing or seeing. We see it from our own unique perspective.

Why not, therefore, engage in dialogue with others with this point clearly in mind? After all, if you challenge them by saying that what they are doing or thinking or saying is wrong, you are clearly only seeing your side of the picture and by saying they are wrong, you instantly engage their defence mechanism. The most obvious result is that they will stand firm and refuse to budge and will probably challenge you back. What results is a verbal bout where no-one has any chance of winning.

Thus if, in all your dealings, you recognise that the strong views offered by your discussant are right from their perspective, and you treat their views with genuine respect, they are likely to treat yours with the same respect. Encourage them to see that both of your views are right from your own perspectives and that if that is so, then you both need to find an accommodating position in which both of you are not only satisfied with the result but will actively work with it in order to move forward.

In my business career I have come across and attended courses on communication and these regularly cover such topics as tolerance, respect, courtesy, flexibility, listening skills, clarity, tone of voice, honesty and more. All of these are relevant and all are important but I have found that as long as I see them as external lessons, they become a little intellectual. I have found that learning from and about myself and my own needs has given me the greatest clarity about what is important.

1) Be Genuine, be honest. Speak from the heart. You can get away with falsehoods for a while but ultimately others will see through the deception and slowly but surely, the level of your credibility as a person will die with it. Once trust has been lost it can of course be regained but it takes an awfully long time. It throws up the question raised earlier in chapter 4 about whether one is living a life of moral duality – one set of morals and values for work and another for home.

2) Be a good listener – everybody has a viewpoint, and to them it is always right. People really want to be heard. To feel heard is to feel valued and validated and nothing matters more to people than feeling valued. Take what they have to say seriously and understand that from their position they are right, even if it screams at you as being wrong. They are far more likely to listen to another point of view if they feel validated first.

3) Be Generous. When I think of my life experiences, those people I have the greatest respect and warmth for have always been generous by nature. Even when you feel anger brewing and a desire to be scathing, be generous. Errors are often made in the heat of the moment and it is always easier to recover from an error if you have been generous.

4) Treat others as you would wish to be treated yourself. Have compassion. Treat everyone with respect, courtesy and as equals. Be tolerant and in particular, be tolerant of their mistakes. Mirror how you would like to be treated yourself in similar circumstances. Compassion embraces kindness, empathy, curiosity without presumptions and of course, presence – just being there for someone.[3]

5) When you speak, keep it simple and speak with clarity and balance. Speak your truth quietly and easily. The less complicated it is, the clearer and more effective it is. Our greatest sages have always communicated their truths quietly and concisely. They always come back to simplicity.

6) Look for mutual interests. In any negotiation or 'discussion' in which you participate, whether at home or at the workplace, always look for mutual interests. How could you both benefit from an agreement? It encourages a different attitude in both you and the other party.

7) Laugh at yourself. The more you connect with your intuitive self, the more you will be able to laugh at yourself. You will no longer need to protect your ego. I love it when people can joke about and laugh at themselves. It reflects a sense of ease with who they really are, no pretences needed, no 'image' to project.

In this day and age of fast moving high-pressured demands at work, it is easy to allow the pressure to invade our communications, both at work and at home. In my experience, taking the time to take several deep breaths to separate myself from the challenges at hand and see them from a 'helicopter' perspective, makes all the difference as to how I then communicate with others (and myself) about them. Sometimes what is needed is a little extra time to think, or for my intuition to throw up some keys to solving these issues.

With Facebook, Google plus, Twitter and other social networking sites, we can communicate with more nations, cultures and people than ever before. The Internet and email now serve a much grander role than we could have imagined 10 years ago, bringing people together in a way that has never happened in the past. Online computer games allow people to come out of their shells and 'be themselves' in ways they would never normally be in public, allowing for extraordinary creativity. Mobile phones have given power to the common man, as has been seen in the leaderless revolutions in the Middle East and Africa, giving them the ability to respond instantly to circumstances. Much is changing and will continue to do so. The communications revolution has only just begun.

Intuitive listening

The danger of such high-tech communication is that it is fast and impersonal. The wording in an email can come over completely differently to the reader than it was meant to and cause real relationship issues. It is thus crucial to keep up real, direct communications, especially when dealing with important issues, as the energy created between the discussants will greatly affect the tone and outcome of the communication. It allows our other senses to not only give but also receive constant signals and this helps us to convey our message and also to feel into the energy of the person with whom we are communicating.

The intuitive self responds to these signals and will quietly give us feedback. A large percentage of us pay no attention until the feeling is so strong that it is almost unavoidable. These feelings are valuable as they tap into the real signals being given off by the person with whom we are communicating. Of course these can be picked up on the phone and even from an email (reading between the lines) but nothing beats real, direct, face-to-face communications.

For some, direct communication is challenging as it engages the egoical self and that may be uncomfortable. The proliferation of blogs tells us that for many, the Internet offers a freedom to communicate their truths in a way that they have not been able to do before and those with similar interests engage with them. Much creativity and original thought comes from these sources so it is useful to keep tapped in to the wider picture as the world moves forward into this new era.

Without dialogue, we cannot move forward effectively and the more genuine we are in our approach, the greater the chances of beneficial success. There are many techniques that are taught, especially in the art of negotiation, all of which are useful but the best negotiators will always be those who work from the heart and who genuinely seek the very best way forward for all concerned.

"The greatest general is the one who wins one thousand battles without fighting."

Sun Tzu - The Art of War

James Maberly

¹*A Poison Tree*

I was angry with my friend:
I told my wrath, my wrath did end.
I was angry with my foe:
I told it not, my wrath did grow.

And I watered it in fears,
Night and morning with my tears;
And I sunned it with smiles,
And with soft deceitful wiles.

And it grew both day and night,
Till it bore an apple bright.
And my foe beheld it shine.
And he knew that it was mine,

And into my garden stole
When the night had veiled the pole;
In the morning glad I see
My foe outstretched beneath the tree.

by William Blake (1757-1827)

²*I studied negotiation under Samuel Passow of the Negotiation Lab,*
and worked with him as an assistant to understand the process better.
I also studied Mediation in London with the Buon Consultancy.

³*The Charter for Compassion was established by Karen Armstrong on*
2008 and is now supported by organisations and people right across
the globe. http://charterforcompassion.org

11
Are you a true or a selfish leader?

"True leaders are hardly known to their followers.
Next after them are the leaders the people know and admire;
After them, those they fear;
After them, those they despise.

To give no trust is to get no trust.

When the work is done right with no fuss or boasting,
All the people say, "We ourselves have achieved it." [1]

Lao-Tzu (sixth century BC)

There is a huge amount of published work on leadership, some of which is very good. What I would like to do is take a more holistic view of leadership as a whole and to recognise that there are approaches to leadership within the developed and the developing worlds which respect and encourage the sovereignty of the individual. It is in recognising the inherent abilities of individuals and nurturing them that we will encourage more rapid progress than a more autocratic style will produce.

I recall as a young man participating in officer selection for the Royal Military Academy of Sandhurst. This was a three day event which involved interviews, logic tests, evaluation exams, public speaking, drama, an individual assault course (to assess common sense) and group tasks in which one person was put in charge of a particular task to be achieved using the whole group, within a specified time. I recall thinking I had blown my logic tests and my evaluation exams, but felt I would succeed in my practical tasks.

In the individual assault course test I had a few minutes to complete as many obstacles as I could and started really badly by falling off the first and landing on my back, completely winding myself. I couldn't breathe! I lay there, gasping for air as the clock was still running. Shortly after I was able to set off again time was called and I had only completed about four of the obstacles. I knew without question that I had failed on that test alone.

Later on in the group tasks, of all eight that were completed by our squad, mine could not have ended at a worse point than it did. Everything I tried failed and when my time was up, the entire group were all still standing on the starting mat. We had gone nowhere and achieved nothing. I now knew for absolute certain that I had failed abysmally. I returned to Catterick (from whence I had come) with my head hung in shame and prepared for the awful news that would follow in a day or two and wondered how I would break the news to my expectant parents.

To my utter astonishment, I had passed. I was so amazed I stood there with my mouth gaping. How could this have happened? Surely it was a mistake? I could not believe it. In fact I was so concerned that an error had been made (and didn't want to be humiliated by being told later that indeed it was an error) that I asked my officer commanding to double check. He did and confirmed that I had passed. What is more, I was the only one out of my squad of eight participants who had.

For several days I seemed to float on a cloud. How could I have passed when I had failed so badly and how did some of the others fail when they appeared to have done so well? This question hung with me for a long time and it was only some time later when I sat with an older and wiser retired army friend that I began to understand why. They were not really interested in whether I completed the tasks or not. They were interested in how I approached the tasks, dealt with the failures, considered new ideas, invited new ideas from others and kept control of an unruly group of people all trying to take over from me. My collapse on the ground winding myself was perhaps a blessing in disguise. I did not panic and try to continue when I was clearly still unable to breathe. I waited till I was in a position to continue (probably speeding up the process of recovery) and then continued as fast as possible, so perhaps this actually helped in the final assessment.

The point I am making here is that often those aspects of leadership that would seem to be the most obvious to all watching from the side-lines are not necessarily the most important. There is much more to leadership than meets the eye.

Who are the leaders around us?

Lao Tzu's simple and beautiful observation quoted above is one of the best I have ever come across in relation to leadership. It explains in a nutshell what true leadership is all about; the ability to inspire others to action without any need to take the credit. It also goes to show how little we have learnt about true and empowering leadership over the last 1600 years, since the majority of the leaders we see around us are those in the second, third and fourth categories (as listed in his quote). With Television, radio, the internet, facebook, twitter and an increasing number of new mediums, we are encouraged to boast about our achievements and keep 'waving our hands in the air' as if we don't, people will forget who we are and that would be a travesty. As Oscar Wilde so eloquently put it, '..*the only thing worse than being talked about is not being talked about'*. This is the ego in full play.

Today, as it has done for as long as we know, ego plays a very large part in the role of leadership. I recall attending a seminar not long ago in which leadership was discussed where the lecturer informed us that to be a successful leader '..*you need a strong ego but that this ego should be qualified by a willingness to be self-effacing'*. This is easier said than done if working from the egoical perspective but is quite correct. Strong or big egos are by nature not self-effacing: they want to be heard and they will structure the way they progress through life in such a way that if they can, they achieve exactly what they want and do so loudly.

It is in taking a 'helicopter view', disengaging from the egoical self and connecting with the intuitive self that we find self-effacement. In this space it is a natural state, rather than having to make a determined effort to be so. This space is accessible to all of us, though not enough of us access it consciously on a regular basis. One notable person who did was Nelson Mandela.

Having spent 27 years in prison, Mandela was catapulted into the limelight both as the world's most famous living person and also as President of the new South Africa. It would have been easy for him to allow the acclaim and the position to go to his head and inflate his ego but he chose differently. He had access to so much power and yet he chose not to use it. Instead, like Ghandi, he empowered others and continued to do so for the remainder of his life.

Leadership roles are generally assumed by those who believe they can lead, most of whom seek success and of course, recognition in the process. Often their position involves some hierarchical status and generally the 'trappings' to go with it. Indeed this approach to leadership is ingrained into our psyches as we grow up.

Far too often a Machiavellian[2] approach to leadership is taken allowing the worst possible egoical traits to blossom. The Machiavellian approach is one of ensuring absolute control, where the end justifies the means. Violence and force are acceptable to stabilize power and one should eliminate political rivals both inside and outside one's own party. It is about gaining and maintaining power at all costs. It proposes that moral corruption is an acceptable and even necessary requirement to achieve stability and security.

It was a shocking revelation to me that so many of our current leaders actively employ this mediaeval approach in their efforts to gain and maintain power. Even more shocking is the knowledge that the young business leaders and politicians of today are being actively encouraged to embrace Machiavelli's teachings in order to succeed.

Rarely does one come across someone like Mandela who does not seek the recognition for what they are doing or have done.

These leaders are simply content that what they have achieved has been effective and that others have benefitted as a result. This is a classic example of servant leadership. Recently I was having a discussion with someone about Lao-Tzu's definition of 'true leadership' and after I had explained it to my listener, she said '... but where is the recognition? How can I show others what I have achieved if I don't advertise it?' Surely it depends entirely on the motivation behind the need. If the need is simply to brag, then it is wrapped in ego. If it is for a CV (résumé), then there is great sense in explaining what you have achieved. Generally those who are quietly effective are very well respected and will have little trouble in progressing along their career paths as their skills in motivating and inspiring others will not go unnoticed.

Servant Leadership

The term 'servant leadership' was coined by Robert Greenleaf and this theory has been supported by many other leadership teachers since then. In his essay 'The Servant as Leader', Greenleaf[3] said:

"It begins with the natural feeling that one wants to serve, to serve first. Then conscious choice brings one to aspire to lead."

Servant Leadership is essentially how many of the most influential people on the planet operated during their lifetimes. Abraham, Jesus Christ, Mohammed, Buddha, Lao-Tzu, Ghandi, Martin Luther King and Nelson Mandela to name but a few. They did not seek the trappings of leadership. Rather, they were focused on helping their fellow men to move forward into a better way of life. Of course it is easy for us to say 'well we are not in that league and as a consequence we simply can't relate to that', but we can most certainly adopt the principles and apply them to whatever we are doing and wherever we are.

Of course there are in every society at the grass roots level, many people who quietly go about their daily lives doing good for others, whether it is helping with old people, youngsters, sports clubs, village Halls, churches or working for such organisations as the Samaritans. These are servant leaders in their own way and they show us a path forward, often shining a bright light on compassion.

Hyrum W. Smith (founder of the Franklin Quest Company) recognised the extraordinary power of servant leadership and wrote about it in an essay in his book 'The 10 Natural Laws of Time and Life Management'. I reprint part of that essay here with his permission as it is very good at explaining in practical terms what servant leadership is all about.

The Servant Leader – by Hyrum W Smith[4]

There is a great deal of overlap between the role of teacher and the role of leader. In fact, some have said that all great leaders are teachers. Why? Because great leaders motivate people to change, to perform at higher levels. That's what both teaching and leadership are all about.

True leaders have power. This is not the power of position or wealth or title. It is more the power of influence, which can only be granted by those who choose to be followers. And because a true leader has this power, it is his or her responsibility to share it, in other words, to empower the followers. And, ironically, you cannot empower people unless they have granted you the power to do so. Then wonderful things happen. This, by the way, is the secret to motivating people. You give them back what they have given you, and the result is synergistic. This is what I call servant leadership. It is simply sharing the abundance of power that you have carried by being their servant rather than their master.

I first discovered this principle when I was in the military. You might think this is a strange place to learn about servant leadership, but that's where I learned it. I soon found that I could not motivate people to do anything unless I was in their physical presence. When I was there, they would do what I wanted them to (because of my position at first, not because I was a true leader), but when I was not present, they would do what they wanted to do. This raised a question in my mind. "What is my role as a leader?" I asked myself. And a little light came on in my mind. The answer was simple: My role as a leader was to create an atmosphere in which my people would do what I wanted them to do - even when I wasn't there - because they wanted to do it. I had to get them to want what I wanted.

When I got into the army, I opted to go to OCS and receive a commission as an officer. The reason I did that was that I wanted to get married, and my wife's father was not excited about his daughter marrying a private in the army. I managed to graduate with honours, so I had my choice of where I wanted to serve in the military. I selected Pershing missiles and was sent to Germany as a Pershing missile commander. I took over a firing battery, with four nuclear warheads, each one thirty-two times bigger than the Hiroshima bomb. We spent thirty days out of every sixty in the fields of Germany with our missiles pointed in the air, aimed at the Eastern Bloc. We had to have the ability to fire those missiles within twelve minutes of being notified that war had broken out.

When I took over this particular unit, the morale was terrible - the commander I replaced had been a West Pointer, he was in it for life and he expected everyone to do what he said, no questions, just do it. One problem with his approach to leadership was that the Pershing missile was a very sophisticated weapon, and many of the people who were brought into the Pershing system were college students. We had a pretty bright group and, quite frankly, they liked to question things. They wanted to know why. At any rate, morale was quite low when I arrived, and on one occasion we were out in the field with our missiles, right out in the open where the Russians would drive by in their cars and take pictures of us. Of course we had our guards out at their posts, but they had to stand there in temperatures that would dip well below zero.

I was platoon commander. I had three officers, who reported to me, then we had a cluster of non-commissioned officers (sergeants), and finally there were the enlisted men—a typical military hierarchy.

And in this structure officers are not supposed to fraternize with the enlisted people. You just don't do that in the military. But I didn't buy into that. While I was out in the field freezing my fanny off, I said, "You know, we ought to build some guard shacks for these guys." And because we had so much to do, there weren't any enlisted people available to build these guard shacks. We had telephone poles lying in this area, and we had a whole bunch of plywood and two-by-fours. But when I suggested that we build these guys some guard shacks, one of the sergeants looked at me and said, "What do you mean, `we'."

I said, "Yeah, let's go build them."

"It's ten below zero out there."

"I don't care how cold it is. Let's go build them."

So I dragged these officers and non-commissioned officers out and we got the telephone poles, cut them off, put them in the ground and built the first shack. About two in the morning we put the first guard in the shack and the guards were absolutely dumbfounded at these officers trying to build shacks for them. We put a little heater in the shack and put up some insulation to keep the cold out. The first one was really bad, but the guards thought it was the Taj Mahal. We improved with experience though and by six o'clock the next night we had four or five finished and all the guards were standing in guard shacks, off the ground, dry and warm.

Well, word passed through the unit quickly, and the morale started to turn around immediately - then an interesting thing began to happen. These guards started looking for things to do, and we got our firing time down to six and a half minutes. About three days later we needed to build a latrine. So in typical military fashion a sergeant 'volunteered' a private from New York City to dig this latrine. This kid had never had a pick in his hand, but he started whacking the ground with it anyway, and it soon became obvious that it was going to take him approximately forever.

I said to him, "Have you ever had a pick in your hand before?"

He said, "Oh, sure, I've had a pick in my hand."

"Well," I said, "let me show you how to use it."

So I took the pick from him and dug about half the latrine. About ten minutes into this we had fifteen guys standing around the edge of this hole watching us. They were absolutely blown away. I had taken my shirt off, so I was just in my T-shirt, and I was having a great time showing this kid how to use a pick. By the time we finished this little lesson, He really did know how to use a pick.

On that particular day some officers from another unit were there, and one of them was a captain.

"You took your shirt off," he said. "Why did you do that?"

"Why did I take my shirt off? You can't dig a trench with a shirt on," I said.

"How's anybody going to know that you're an officer without your shirt on?"

I looked at him and said, "You know, if I have to wear that crummy bar on my lapel so that people will know I'm an officer, then I've got a real problem."

This guy missed the whole point. In his mind, the only way he was able to show his authority was by a small insignia. And in my opinion, if that's the only way you can let your people know you've got authority, you've lost. They're not going to follow you anywhere. What a leader does is get people to do things because they want to, not because they have to. Digging that latrine trench and building those guard shacks made a difference and the morale turned around, because of the message sent by the actions. They got the message loud and clear that the people at the top cared about the people at the bottom of the traditional military hierarchy. We were willing to get physically involved in doing something for them, and they then decided to return the favour. The real lesson I learned from this experience is that if you take care of the people below you, they'll take care of you, and that's important, because your success is dependent on the success of the people under you.

There is a causal relationship between self-worth and productivity and there is nothing that makes people feel greater self-worth than having leaders who go out of their way to serve them. In short, if you want to get greater productivity out of people, serve them, don't exercise dominion over them.

All managers have one type of authority through their positions. But that authority is largely ineffective if it is used to manipulate and push people. No-one who uses authority in this manner has an abundance of power. Servant leaders, on the other hand, may not even have the authority of position, but they will have an abundance of real power, real influence with people, because they have earned it. Their followers have given it to them. When you are entrusted with that kind of power, you have an obligation to share it, to empower others.

One thing we need to remember as we consider the issue of power is that when people grant us power and we have developed the ability to lead, leadership becomes a two-edged sword. A statement I heard long ago (I am not sure where) which has had a great impact on me is as follows: "The power to lead is the power to mislead. The power to mislead is the power to destroy."

As leadership skills are developed and strengthened, we must remember that leadership can also be used for evil. Hitler was probably one of the greatest leaders the world has ever seen, but he used that leadership ability to destroy. George Washington was a magnificent leader. He used his leadership ability to build, lift and create. Leadership carries with it a great responsibility; the responsibility to lift others, to empower them to do more with their lives than they otherwise would be able to. That is the mark of a true leader, one who understands the abundance mentality.

There are many different styles of leadership but Servant Leadership is the style that most embodies Lao-Tzu's concept of true leadership best of all. It is the one that demands the least amount of ego driven action and encourages a holistic view of not only a leader's task, but also their role within the organisation and especially in relation to those whom they would call their followers.

Some examples of Servant Leaders

There are many examples of servant leaders and some very obvious ones (as already explained) but by their very nature, often they are hard to spot. They are quietly effective. Their lives are geared towards serving others with as little fanfare as possible. I have chosen two people whose styles of leadership I consider fit directly into Lao Tzu's definition of True Leadership.

David Coltart is a Zimbabwean Senator. He is the only white member of a Government run by a President who frequently lambasts the white community in Zimbabwe and who has personally and publically denounced David on at least two occasions in the past. David currently holds the post of Minister for Education, Sport, Arts and Culture. He is a lawyer by trade.

Ever since his return from University in Cape Town as a young lawyer, David's activities have been focused on human rights issues, taking on challenging human rights cases. He also established a legal aid clinic for local people who could not afford the services of a lawyer (there is no state-funded legal aid in Zimbabwe). He is not by nature a self-publicist, but as a consequence of standing up for Justice at a time when there were heavy abuses of power by those running the country, he drew considerable attention to himself. As a politician, he is a member of the Movement for Democratic Change and it is under the auspices of the current Prime Minister, Morgan Tsvangirai and the Deputy Prime Minister Arthur Mutambara, that David has been given this Ministerial role.

The country's education sector was in tatters when he assumed the role and despite the fact that there is still very little money available, he and his team have been able to galvanise the educational sector. It is a continuous struggle, especially in a country where there is a very low GDP and most of the funds required for the educational sector come from external donors. Teachers are still paid a pathetically low wage, school buildings are falling into disrepair and many parents cannot afford to pay for their children's school fees, so there are still extraordinary challenges ahead.

As a politician and as a Minister, David has no alternative but to be in the public eye. It is notable that after the establishment of the Government of National Unity, when the newly appointed ministers were asked what type of car they would like to fulfil their roles, whilst others ordered the top-of-the-range vehicles, David settled for a more practical 4 by 4 vehicle which could take him to rural schools. He is quietly determined to play a significant part in the rebuilding of a new democratic nation. He is consistent in his views and actions and whilst he has come under severe criticism from the ZANU PF regime for these views, he is highly respected by all for what he has done with the educational sector and for his considerable efforts at bringing Zimbabwean sport back onto the world stage.

Whilst he is not a pacifist, he believes that we are too quick to jump to military solutions when perhaps dialogue is better called for, but equally that we have been pathetically slow to move when real intervention was necessary, as for example during the genocide in Rwanda. He has a strong belief in the sovereignty of the individual which is reflected in the following statement made in a speech on Religion and Freedom in July 2011 to the 'Centre for Independent Studies' in Australia. David is a Christian.

"By the church, I don't refer to the physical church of historical times and of today, but rather to the body of all the individual people who have put their trust in Christ over the ages. The church is comprised of those who place their trust in Christ, not the physical Institutions created by man... I fear that the very institutions of the church sometimes work to undermine Christ's teachings..."

It is also a recognition that Institutions of every kind, no matter how well founded or well meaning, can be manipulated and controlled by those with different, twisted and sometimes unworthy agendas to lead their followers in a direction that they have chosen. I comment on such 'control' in chapter 5.

He does not actively seek recognition for his work. His motivation is one of serving others and giving those who cannot be heard, a voice. He has strong personal integrity and does not waver from his personal values. He recognises that there are times when, in the recognition that a peaceful solution is the wisest way forward that one must eat, drink and dialogue with those that currently hold power in an effort to create a forward momentum. This is not a decision most people could sit easily with, but it is his firm personal belief in himself and his spiritual faith that give him the presence of mind and strength to participate in such a challenging venture and at such a challenging time.

Michael Young is a British businessman and consultant who started his career as a political advisor to Sir Alec Douglas-Home, British Foreign Secretary, and then to Sir Edward Heath, Britain's Prime Minister.

After graduating from the University of York in PPE in 1972, he moved to ARC Ltd (a stone quarrying company) and then to its parent, Consolidated Gold Fields as Public Affairs Director where he worked under the Chairman, Rudolph Agnew.

Whilst working for Consolidated Gold Fields which has considerable assets in South Africa, Michael became aware of the stalemate between the apartheid regime and the black nationalists and realised that little effort was being made to bring the two sides together to create an opportunity for dialogue. He managed to convince Agnew that this was a necessary process which Agnew agreed to back secretly, but only on the understanding that if it were ever brought into the public eye, he would personally deny it and Michael would be fired.

First of all Michael met with the leader of the ANC, Oliver Tambo. He asked Tambo what his company could do to help resolve the situation. After some thought, Tambo said "I want you to help me build a bridge to Pretoria."

Clearly, they were willing to give the process a try. Then, at considerable risk to himself and his family, Michael set about finding a group of Afrikaners (mainly academics) who were close to the government and would be prepared to begin the process of dialogue with the ANC. While establishing these links, he was regularly followed by South African intelligence agents. His phone was tapped and he sometimes received threatening phone calls at his home.

Over five years, Michael organised and chaired fourteen secret meetings at Mells Park House in Somerset, England. During that period, over and above the core group, new and different people appeared at the meetings bringing new and interesting viewpoints. The South African government, at first taking a suspiciously distant viewpoint on the meetings, began to recognise the importance of this dialogue and increasingly became more responsive to the process.

The meetings were very successful and culminated in the agreement between both sides to meet officially for the first time without conditions. Nelson Mandela was released from prison during the final meeting and they all watched the process live on TV together.

With all the hype and excitement of the release of Nelson Mandela, the birth of a new South Africa and the well-publicised Truth and Reconciliation Commission, no-one noticed Michael's efforts except those who were directly involved and knew what had been taking place. As Willie Esterhuyse (the leader of the Afrikaner contingent) left Mells Park House for the last time he said to Michael, "It takes a big man to remain invisible."

These talks remained almost invisible until the publication of Robert Harvey's book, 'The Fall of Apartheid'. Channel 4 then financed the production of the excellent film 'Endgame' about the dialogue process. Had this not happened, Michael Young's achievements would have remained mostly hidden from view.

In 2001 he was granted an OBE for his contribution to human rights. He does not wear this on his sleeve and it took me some searching to discover that he had in fact been recognised for his work. He is a very self-effacing man and appears somewhat embarrassed when discussing this aspect of his life. He is a classic example of a Servant Leader.

Michael had built up some remarkable friendships during that period and even today these friendships remain and he continues to take an interest in events in Southern Africa with his work as an advisor and consultant.

In a comment at the end of Michael's interview on the Channel 4 website is the following comment from Crimson Tazvinzwa made on 5th May 2009.

"Watching the documentary 'Endgame' was a reminder to me and many others that good and selfless people like Michael Young do actually exist. Against all the odds and scepticism around at the time, Mr Young was able to sustain one of the most difficult but important political dialogues of our time; and sure enough the reward of hard work and persistence did not disappoint; a new South Africa (rainbow nation) was born. I hope there are still many more Michael Young's out there because as we speak, Zimbabwe, once a bread basket of the Southern African region needs men and women with vision and foresight."[5]

In summing up these two characters (David Coltart and Michael Young) and the roles they are playing/have played, one might be tempted to consider that there is something different about them, something that the majority of us don't have. I would argue that we all have the ability to undertake roles with a similar challenge and there are many out there doing extraordinary things. The primary reason these men have acted in the way they have is as follows;

a) They have been able to extract themselves from 'group think' or the 'herd mentality' (being tied to rules of 'normality') on so many issues that might have stopped them. They are therefore following their own rules.

b) They have a greater link with their intuitive selves as a

117

consequence and are less driven by the egoical filter than the majority of us. This allows for the quiet confidence that is needed to perpetuate such demanding roles.

c) They have followed something they feel passionate about, an issue which drives them forward. We all have a driving force within us. Whether we 'find' it and do anything with it depends on whether we allow ourselves the privilege of doing so.

It is our willingness to participate in this process which makes the difference. Some start earlier than others but many people make entries along the route at all ages and have an extraordinary impact on the lives of those around them.

Servant leadership and cultivating creativity

Servant leadership in itself does not require such dramatic commitments but it is a state of mind which embodies the same principles. By 'serving' those you lead, at the very least you offer them respect. This in turn encourages them to think better of themselves and of what they do. As Hyrum Smith suggests in his essay, the more you do for them, the more they will do for you.

A servant leader is thus in an extraordinary position in that he or she already has the respect of those they lead and in that capacity has the power to influence them creatively. The more we connect with our intuitive selves, the more we act from a position of balance, without selfishness and without moral duplicity.

As trusted leaders, we are in an extraordinary position to encourage people to step back and re-examine their lives, their attitudes, their belief systems and their raison d'être and to engage in a way that will enhance not only their own lives but also those of others around them at the same time.

Helping others to recognise the power of their intuition and begin the process of cultivating original thoughts has to be a powerful idea. We need creative people now more than ever and team leaders more than anyone else should recognise this.

This does not mean that everyone has to find something

dramatic to achieve. It may mean simply that in being more themselves and less 'driven' by external rules and their egoical selves, they are able to be more creative and perhaps even encourage others (including their children) into looking at themselves in a new and more creative way. Maybe that is enough. One never knows quite where it might lead.

"After they arrived at Capernaum and settled in a house, Jesus asked his disciples, "What were you discussing out on the road?" But they didn't answer, because they had been arguing about which of them was the greatest. He sat down, called the twelve disciples over to him, and said, "Whoever wants to be first must take last place and be the servant of everyone else."

Mark, Chapter 9 vs 33-35, The Bible

[1] *Original text: 'The highest type of ruler is one of whose existence the people are barely aware. Next comes one whom they love and praise. Next comes one whom they fear. Next comes one whom they despise and defy. When you are lacking in faith, others will be unfaithful to you. The Sage is self-effacing and scanty of words. When his task is accomplished and things have been completed, all the people say, 'We ourselves have achieved it!'*
Tao Te Ching, attributed to Lao-Tzu

[2] *Niccolò Machiavelli (1469–1527) was an Italian historian, politician, diplomat, philosopher, humanist, and writer based in Florence during the Renaissance. Around 1513, he circulated a book entitled 'The Prince' which was a philosophical treatise on leadership in Government in which he maintains that gaining and maintaining power by whatever means necessary is critical to on-going political survival. Alan Yentob*

produced an excellent programme for the BBC entitled 'Whose afraid of Machiavelli' at this link
https://www.youtube.com/watch?v=sMkt1Vq7tJ4&feature=kp

[3] *The Robert Greenleaf Centre for Servant Leadership, which continues to promote Robert Greenleaf's work, holds an annual conference in June in Indianapolis. The Centre can be found at the following link; http://www.greenleaf.org.*

[4] *Hyrum W. Smith was the founder of the Franklin Quest Company. In 1997 it amalgamated with the Covey Leadership Centre, forming FranklinCovey which remains today one of the leading leadership training organisations in the USA,*

[5] *Source of comment from Crimson Tazvinzwa made on 05 May 2009. (From channel 4) http://www.channel4.com/programmes/endgame/articles/the-real-michael-young*

Why Follow Rules?

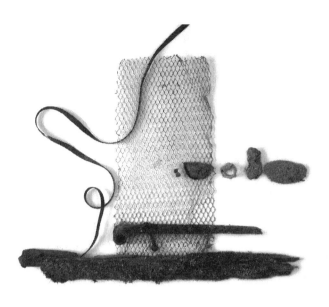

Intuitive drawing with found objects by Jillifar Amor

12

What is your passion?

"Don't ask yourself what the world needs; ask yourself what makes you come alive. And then go and do that. Because what the world needs is people who have come alive."
Dr Howard Thurman, Author, theologian and Philosopher

The seven previous questions are focused on who we are, how we can better operate and how we respond to others. They boil down to two important and critical factors:

a) We need to recognise that life has placed us in a metaphorical tunnel. What we learn of our history extends the tunnel backwards and the rules and perceptions we live by strengthen the sides of the tunnel and extend it ahead of us. Thus we can only see forwards or backwards. What is to our left and our right, above and below is not visible to us at all. Thus a myriad of exciting potentials and opportunities are lost to us unless we can break away from the rules and structures, release the anchors of history and move up to the end of the tunnel. From there, the view is exquisite. Every possible potential is available to us and we can head off in any direction we want, unencumbered by all our previous ties.

b) Our recognition of and engagement with the intuitive self shows us there is another side to us, quite separate from the egoical self. It frees us to be ourselves, powered from within rather than powered from without. The ego feeds off the external and clogs up the mind with its incessant chatter, dominating our thought processes and thus becoming the major influence in our lives. The intuitive self on the other hand is quiet, non-judgemental and creative and comes from the heart. It is who we really are. Allowing the intuitive self to be our guide will radically change our perspective on life.

The final question brings all of the other questions together, as the key to cultivating original thoughts is having a reason to do so in the first place. What is driving us? What is it we feel passionate about?

Passion can be stimulated by a whole array of different ideas and many great things have been achieved and accomplished. Passion however is not limited to achieving something tangible. Your passion could be one of exploration, of curiosity, of seeking enlightenment or freedom. Einstein once wrote "I have no special talents. I am only passionately curious." Whatever it is that stimulates your own inner passion is enough.

It may be that, when you question yourself about this, you can't actually put your finger on what drives you. If this is where you are, consider some of your natural traits. What interests you most? What will you travel a long way to do? What programmes do you watch and what books do you read? They may give you an indication of what it is that really interests you. If still nothing emerges, don't panic. Engage with the other seven questions and in time, slowly but surely, your real passion will emerge.

What are your dreams? Often we have dreams that come to us in our quiet moments, such as sitting on the beach, lying in the bath or walking in the mountains, at moments when we are closely in touch with the intuitive self. It may be that your core dream is drowned out by the ego distracting you by swamping your consciousness, demanding that you do things that expand your external credibility. When it really is from the heart, all else becomes unimportant compared to the passion itself.

Temporary passions

Don't be confused by temporary passions or drives which may

serve you for any number of reasons at any particular time. They may be very important at that moment but unless they come from the heart, they will ultimately dissipate.

I recall when I was at school I was in a particular rugby team (rugby football) playing as a lock forward. I enjoyed rugby but I have never been naturally aggressive. If however I became angry in a game, woe betide anyone in my way. During one match, someone hit me in the face and from that moment on I was a dynamo. It happened again in the next match. Then the next, and the next. It occurred to me that this was becoming a little repetitive, so I watched for it in the next game. To my surprise, I discovered it was someone in my own team punching me, not the opposition. I was furious, and after the game I demanded an explanation.

"You come alive once you're angry" they responded, "so we always give you a punch just to wake you up!" In effect it was a temporary passion, driven by a desire to 'get my own back' on the opposition (poor chaps!).

For others it may be to generate an immediate income or help a school raise funds for a new swimming pool, or build a village Hall for the local community. These are temporary passions and, whilst strong at the time, may not be your own core passion. If you work for a company, your boss may infuse you with his/her own passion and encourage you to find yours within the company's framework. That is likely not to be your main driving force. If on the other hand you love the specific type of work that you are doing, then it doesn't matter which company you work for, as long as they allow you to indulge your passion.

I have a friend, Tom Benyon[1] who at 72 has walked over 1000 miles across England and has raised nearly a million pounds in the process of doing so. He is passionate about the work of the charity he runs but it is more than that. It has become part of who he is.

Passions can develop as a result of having a child who struggles with school or having a close friend or relative who dies of cancer or some other debilitating illness. It really doesn't matter what kindles the initial spark. If it comes from deep within you, from your heart, then it will infuse you with an energy that will propel you forward, often in a way that you never imagined possible.

Mahatma Ghandi

Ghandi is revered by people across the world for his stand in India against British Occupation and for his earlier protests in South Africa for the rights of all Indians. He led India to Independence and inspired movements for non-violence across the globe.

When we consider what he achieved, we cannot imagine that at any time he could have been a somewhat ineffectual and shy individual. Yet during his school days he showed no really promising signs either in the classroom or on the field and was described as a mediocre student, passing his exams with some difficulty. He studied law in London at the behest of his parents which exposed him to many new ideas and concepts but on his return to India, his efforts to set up a law practice failed abysmally as he was too shy to speak up in court. He resorted to modest work drafting petitions for litigants – effectively back office activity.

It was when he moved to South Africa that his passion was aroused. He took a job working for Muslim Indian Traders based in Pretoria. Having been educated as a barrister in England where he was treated as an equal, he found he immediately became a victim of discrimination in South Africa, his first experience of which was being thrown off a train for sitting in First Class accommodation on his way to Pretoria. Ghandi was deeply shaken by the way Indians were treated and it sparked a determination in him to overcome the injustice being perpetrated under British rule. Once he had the bit between his teeth, nothing was going to stop him. Infused with passion and determined to act with non-violent protest and rooting his actions in truth, he engineered some truly remarkable changes, not only for South Africa and India but also for the world.

Betty Makoni

Betty Makoni[2] comes from Zimbabwe. At the age of six, she was brutally raped. At the age of nine, her mother died as a result of domestic violence, forcing her to take on the role of mother to her other siblings. As a teenager, she began to realise that the horror she had suffered was widespread and that most women simply accepted it as part of their lot. Betty thought differently. She determined then at that youthful age that she would make a difference for all the women in Africa who suffered as she did; and so her passion was born.

She educated herself, paying for her own schooling and then went on to University where she was awarded two degrees. On returning home and seeing that nothing had changed, she set up a support network locally for girls who had been raped or physically abused. This extended more widely until by 2006 there were 30,000 girls who belonged to some 500 'clubs' around the country.

After challenging President Robert Mugabe publically about the abusive actions of his renegade youth militia, she was forced to leave the country. She was nominated for the CNN Hero award along with 900 others and is one of only a few who have won the accolade. Today, she is leader of the Girl Child Network Worldwide which has grown from the ten female students from her class in Zimbabwe to millions of girls worldwide, making it one of the largest global movements for girls. She has received countless awards for her selfless service to downtrodden women and continues to work at the rock face.

None of this would have happened if she had not had a passionate urge to make a change, and one that has driven her since her youth. Passion is what makes the difference between mediocre effort and determined progress.

So allow your passion space to breathe. If you already know what it is, then give yourself permission to live it. If you live what it is that you truly love doing, it ceases to be 'work' in the laborious sense of the word. Your passion will create the determination you need to see it through. When doubt creeps in as it inevitably will, remind yourself of why you are following this path and re-ignite the passion. Not only will it be fulfilling but it will bring you joy and you will find you have more energy than you ever imagined possible to make it happen.

"Don't worry about your originality. Set yourself as free as you can and your originality will take care of you. What I would say to you is to watch your work mighty well and see that it is the voice that comes from within you that speaks in your work."

Robert Henri: artist and teacher, 1865-1929. 'The Art Spirit', 1984

[1] *Tom Benyon is the Chief Executive of the charity ZANE (Zimbabwe, a National Emergency) which has been assisting old people of all races to survive after their savings were obliterated by the collapse of the local Zimbabwean currency. ZANE is also pioneering a model for the redevelopment and regeneration of local communities who are currently in crisis. www.zane.uk.com*

[2] *Betty Makoni runs the Girl Child Network Worldwide, now based in London, which operates across the globe. She has recently released her autobiography 'Never Again', a very powerful story of how she determined to stand up and make a difference in the lives of women in Africa. www.girlchildnetworkworldwide.org.*

Visit **www.cultivating-intuition.com** *for more background, links to talks, images, references and a regular blog of new ideas.*

Part 3

Those who have broken the mold

"The intellect has little to do on the road to discovery. There comes a leap in consciousness, call it intuition or what you will, and the solution comes to you and you don't know how or why."

Albert Einstein

James Maberly

Intuitive 3D drawing with found objects by JoJo Maberly aged 11

13

Those who have broken the mold

"As for the future, your task is not to foresee it but to enable it".
Antoine De Saint-Exupery

I remember when I was a child growing up, the last day of the school holidays meant a trip to the barber. There was always a queue of kids sitting there patiently awaiting their turn for a haircut. There was no choice of style; it was always short back and sides all round. Everyone headed off to school with the same hairstyle. Forced conformity.

Today things are different. Choice exists (which is a huge step forward) but what we tend to choose are the hairstyles and clothes of our peer group. Why do we do this? Clearly because we feel more comfortable being a part of the 'club'. We invest a great deal of time and energy in ensuring our friends see us as 'part of the team'. We believe it gives us a sense of identity when actually it is doing the exact opposite. In molding ourselves to the collective personality, we distance ourselves from who we really are.

Many years ago I lived for a short while in a squat in London. One of my 'housemates' was a great hulk of a chap who was a skinhead. He was part of a gang who roamed the streets hassling people and causing trouble. He was covered in chains and was very intimidating to look at. I discovered after about a week that he was actually rather a shy gentle chap who had had a hard time at school and hated having been in that position. So desperate was he not to be the unwitting victim of these gangs himself that he had changed his persona and had become one of them. In the house he was one person; with the gang, he was someone completely different.

This is the ego at work and behind the 'pleasure' or 'validation' of being seen as part of the group is a haunting fear of being rejected. Why else would one need to conform so dramatically? I have often watched this over the years in our children as they prepare for a party or a day out with friends. They go through agonies deciding what to wear, what is cool and what is un-cool. Our attempts to help are often shot down with lines like "you don't understand! Leave me alone!"

We accept that all children go through this stage to some degree (it is all part of discovering more about themselves) but regrettably the vast percentage of the population never really move on from this stage until perhaps later in life.

So choice exists and yet we choose to conform. Weird, is it not?

Mold breakers

Luckily for us there are some who have decided to follow a path they have personally chosen, whether it fits with the norms of society or not. They are our leaders. Some have become very wealthy in the process whilst others still earn next to nothing and yet they are still our leaders. They are the ones guiding us forward and opening our eyes to new possibilities. They are the ones who stand out like lighthouses, shining a light on the route ahead.

So what is it they are showing us? Is it how to establish and market tools for mass communication, create immense wealth, paint a picture, play a cello or how to recover from an addiction to alcohol? Yes indeed it is all of these, but each of these 'functions' or 'actions' is but a small part of the message. The real part is in showing us that by engaging with the intuitive self, our own real inner core, we find inside that we are more than we could ever have imagined. We are extraordinary, we are exceptionally able and we don't have to try to be like anyone else. We just need the courage to be ourselves and step up to and over the line.

I have chosen to write about five individuals from very different walks of life; four are still alive but alas, one is no longer with us. Each of them stands out as someone who has stepped across the line. For a couple of them it appears to have been reasonably easy but for others the journey has been paved with pain, anxiety and self-doubt. How the journey has been accomplished is both fascinating and revealing but it is where they are now (or where they ended up) that makes the difference. When you read the following chapters, use your senses to feel into their energy. See if you can extract from the pages the wisdom written between the lines. That is where the real learning will be.

Often the questions put to those interviewed are roughly the same and purposely so in order to see how and if their approaches to life coincide. They provide a great insight into the lives of all five of these people and in particular the key drivers behind what they do or have done. Ultimately what you take from these chapters and how receptive you are to the information contained in them will be entirely up to you.

There are many others who have stepped across the line whom I could have interviewed. All of us know people who fit into this category but we don't often stop to consider what makes the difference between them and the others around them. Hopefully these chapters will help to provide some insight into what makes them tick. You may find that in reading their stories, you recognise how far down your track you already are and perhaps, just perhaps, it will give you the inspiration to take that step across the line – and keep walking.

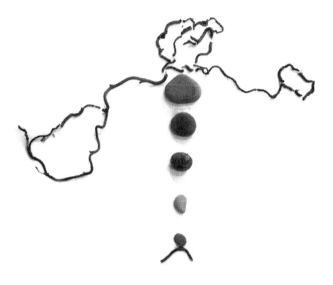

Intuitive drawing using found objects by JoJo Maberly aged 11

14

Steve Jobs – a lifetime of advice in a single paragraph

"Your time is limited, so don't waste it living someone else's life. Don't be trapped by dogma, which is living with the results of other people's thinking. Don't let the noise of others' opinions drown out your own inner voice and most important, have the courage to follow your heart and intuition. They somehow already know what you truly want to become. Everything else is secondary."

Steve Jobs - 'How to live before you die', Stanford University, 2005 [1]

Steve Jobs

In his speech **'How to live before you die'** at Stanford University in 2005, Steve Jobs spoke of dropping 'out' of college when he could see no value in continuing what he was doing, trusting that it would all work out OK. He reflected on how it was one of the best decisions he ever made. Whilst he had officially dropped out he stayed on at University, sleeping on the floor in his friends' rooms and following his intuition, he dropped 'in' to those classes he wanted to attend. At the time he could see no specific reason for dropping in, just an inkling that it was the right thing to do. It proved to be invaluable later.

Some ten or so years later after starting Apple, the year after the launching of the very first Mac, he lost his job at Apple. At first he was devastated but he later realised that it was the best thing that ever happened to him. He started up 'Next' and then 'Pixar Animations' which went on to become the most successful animation studio in the world.

Not long after this, 'Next' was bought by Apple and he found himself back in the Apple family, and the heart of Apple's renaissance is based on what he and his team had developed at 'Next.'

What is clear about Steve Jobs is that he had a passion for what he did and he hired people who had a passion for what they could do. He knew it was a critical ingredient for an individual's continued growth and development.

"I am convinced that the only thing that kept me going was that I loved what I did. You've got to find what you love...do what you believe is great work, and the only way to do great work is to love what you do. If you haven't found it yet, keep looking, and don't settle. As with all matters of the heart, you will know when you have found it...and it gets better and better as the years roll on, so keep looking – don't settle."[2]

Death – an extraordinary motivator

Steve Jobs found that recognising that he could die at any moment was extraordinarily liberating. He found that in consciously engaging with it and really feeling that death might be round the corner, all external expectations, pride and the fear of embarrassment or failure fell away. It simply didn't matter anymore and left only what was truly important to focus on.

"Remembering that you are going to die is the best way I know to avoid the trap of thinking you have something to lose. You are already naked. There is no reason not to follow your heart."[3]

As he reached the end of the talk, Steve made the observations quoted at the start of the chapter. This is a very powerful statement and deserves serious contemplation as it contains so much wisdom in a very short paragraph. It is actually not one message but five, melded together into a perfect package. I will break these down into sub-paragraphs as each message should be considered separately.

"Your time is limited, so don't waste it living someone else's life."

How many of us spend our lives working for someone else, doing whatever it is that they want us to do? Sure, they provide us with an income and there are a multitude of reasons why we should stick with this sometimes soul-destroying existence, but there is a question that begs to be answered; have we given up the opportunity to do something with our own lives which would make our hearts sing? Of course there are many who love working for others and find their jobs extremely fulfilling which is wonderful as clearly their dreams and desires (beyond the wallet) are being met. If it is only for the wallet, then the entire motivation of their lives is built on a false premise and it is likely they will end their days justifying their wealth to themselves whilst feeling emptiness inside and wondering, 'what was it all for?'

Sir Ken Robinson[4], a leading authority on education explained in a recent talk that the majority of people he meets do not really enjoy what they do and see their work simply as a means to an end.

He also meets people who clearly love what they do and couldn't imagine doing anything else with their lives as it speaks of who they are. His concern is that not enough people fit into this category.

The message is clear. If you really want to get fulfilment out of your life, then contemplate your dreams, your deep desires. What is it that inspires you, that excites you more than anything else? If you were asked what it is that you would most like to do for the rest of your life, what would it be? Be sure not to discount your thoughts on the basis of 'oh that's impossible' or 'I could never do that'. Allow yourself the sheer privilege of freeing up enough to contemplate what really makes your heart sing. If the desire to do it wells up from inside you, then it is heartfelt. If on the other hand it is a reasoned idea and all the dots join up and intellectually it looks like a perfect scenario, it won't be a heartfelt pleasure and no matter how much money you might make from the venture, you will only be able to say to yourself that you are DOING. Until you can say you are BEING, it will always ultimately prove unsatisfactory.

"Don't be trapped by dogma, which is living with the results of other people's thinking."

Here Steve Jobs recognises how easy it is to become trapped in the dogma of others, to grow up in an environment in which the doctrines of those around you become the 'norm' and which you do not question. We see this all over the world in every society. In the study of negotiation it is considered one of the areas most difficult to encourage people to shift from as adherence to dogma is generally rigid and seen as truth.

Regrettably this is where so many religions have become wedged. In so many cases, the simple and beautiful messages imparted by the great teachers have become manipulated to suit the desires of those in control. The very fact that there are over 300 different variations of the Church in the USA suggests that there is an awful lot of dogma being preached as if it were truth.

Dogma exists in almost all areas of our lives and in particular, politics, culture and social society. It could be argued that for every dogma that exists there is a counter dogma. What Jobs is suggesting is exactly what Buddha proposed; don't just simply accept anything as truth – question it. Indeed, do not simply accept the writings in this book - question them. Work out for yourselves what you personally believe. Feel into these concepts. If you can free yourself up enough to take a good 'helicopter' view, you will find you have an intuitive knowing about whether something is wrong or right for you. It is only from this vantage point that you can determine what is right for you.

As children reach their final years in school, perhaps it should become mandatory for them to have regular discussions in which they are led through a series of questions about life and 'normal' perceptions, i.e. dogma. Debates should be held where pupils are asked to represent opposing or differing views to their own. This type of dialogue helps to widen people's perceptions of life and helps them to ask questions of themselves and the 'norms' in their lives. They help to encourage pupils to look at things from a 'helicopter' perspective and start setting their own boundaries and guidelines, separate from the external influences around them.

"Don't let the noise of others' opinions drown out your own inner voice"

There are many people who enter our lives who seem so sure about what it is they are speaking of and in our uncertainty we listen to and feed off them. Their clarity provides comfort to our dependent and searching selves and our voices can be very easily drowned out by their loud and confident ministrations. We ourselves often enter into the process of quietening our own voices and sometimes we might even become vehicles for spouting their dogmas as if they were our own.

I have several friends whom I love dearly who all have one thing in common. Most of what they do or say is directed at covering their own insecurities. They are often highly motivated people who sound extraordinarily convincing and motivate many others to work with them but they cannot abide being questioned or challenged. They simply cannot cope with it and rather than take a 'helicopter' perspective and review what has been said, they prefer to ambush whatever it is that causes them to feel insecure. One moment a particular person may be their 'greatest friend', the next they are 'persona non grata' for having challenged something to which they are very anchored.

Take time to listen to your own voice. Remember the old Irish adage, *'How can I know what I think until I hear what I say?'* Just because you are the only one who is not in agreement doesn't mean you are wrong. Remember what you have read about the concept of 'group think' and the 'herd mentality'. Allow your own voice to be heard. If the thought of speaking out is terrifying, then start the process of finding your intuitive self. Begin to connect with who you really are; set your own guidelines and write your views down. That at least is a great starting point.

"...and most important, have the courage to follow your heart and intuition. They somehow already know what you truly want to become."

I could not have said it better myself.

One thing I would add here is that what you may finally end up doing may not be the initial work your heart leads you to do but whatever it is, throw your heart and soul into it. Go with it. Allow yourself to run with your intuition and you will surprise yourself with the results. Sometimes, everyone and everything may be screaming at you NOT to follow your heart for any number of 'good' reasons. Consider them all carefully and make your own decisions but don't forget that ultimately, you have to live whatever life you choose and live with yourself in the process.

"Everything else is secondary."

And so it is. This is a little like the last two words of Christ's teaching 'Love thy neighbour **as thyself'**. They seem unimportant at first, but actually they colour the picture of the whole statement. Those who have stepped out and done something with their lives have recognised this clearly. They know what they want to do and they do it with passion.

This does not mean we obliterate everything else from our lives. We all have to eat and sleep and participate in life, but if we do it our way with our dreams, knowing that what we do is a result of our inner-most desires and motivations, then not only do we grow in confidence and wisdom, we also have an authenticity about us that speaks volumes to those around us. It will speak to our children, to our friends, to those we teach and to our associates in a way that words can never convey.

Steve Jobs stepped out of the mold. Despite his somewhat disjointed childhood (he was an adopted child) he discovered his intuitive self, set his own boundaries, freed himself from dogma and recognised that he did not have to rely on external structures and influences. He was comfortable with who he was and recognised his own greatness, in the way that we should all see our own greatness; by listening to our intuition and having the courage to step out and follow our hearts.

The regrets of the dying

When their lives draw to a close, many old people seem to develop a clarity of perception and when questioned about what they would have done differently in their lives, regular themes appeared. Here are some of their common regrets.

a) I wish I had done what I wanted and not what others wished me to do.
b) I wish I hadn't worked so hard.
c) I wish I'd had the courage to be myself.
d) I wish that I had enjoyed myself more.

Consider how many of these are the antithesis of what Steve Jobs is proposing. There are clearly many lessons not just to be learnt but also to be applied if we are to live our lives more effectively.

He also had something else to say in the same speech which is critically important if you are to take the leap forward and follow your own dreams. Here is why. Sometimes the way forward that you choose may seem rather pointless or perhaps irrelevant in the grand scheme of things, especially when the issue of generating an income comes into play. You have to trust that it will all work out in the end.

"You can't connect the dots looking forwards (being the many things you will have learnt and done along the way), you can only connect them looking backwards...You have to trust in something; your gut, destiny, life, karma, whatever, because believing that the dots will connect down the road will give you the confidence to follow your heart, even when it leads you off the well-worn path, and that will make all the difference."[5]

We do not have to become successful heads of large corporations. Neither do we have to invent something that changes the world. It may be that all we need to do is relax into being who we really are and the authenticity we then project as we speak and mix with others provides them with the necessary wisdom to get up and follow their own hearts. In effect, we become teachers of BEING rather than DOING. Some of our greatest teachers are those we come across in life whether friends, family, work colleagues or strangers whose presence and conduct has a

profound effect upon us.
Achieving that would truly be a success.

1,2,3,5 *The link to the Stanford University speech by Steve Jobs is as follows: http://www.youtube.com/watch?v=D1R-jKKp3NA*

4 *Sir Kenneth Robinson (Liverpool, 4 March 1950) is an English author, speaker, and international advisor on education in the arts to government, non-profits, education, and arts bodies. He was Director of The Arts in Schools Project (1985–89), Professor of Arts Education at the University of Warwick (1989–2001), and was knighted in 2003 for services to education.*

Visit **www.cultivating-intuition.com** *for more background, links to talks, images, references and a regular blog of new ideas.*

15

Scott Russell – from jewellery repair to multi-millionaire

Scott Russell

Scott Russell has a vibrant energy about him. He exhibits a determination that clearly shows how and why he has achieved what he has up until now.

Scott was born in Essex into an entrepreneurial family. His parents were market traders, his mother designing and making jewellery whilst his father had a fencing business. He grew up understanding two important points; that a good business is something you enjoy doing and which makes you money. He worked on the market stall from the age of eight and could cash up by the time he was ten. He found school a waste of time, particularly maths. He challenged his teachers by asking how this could help him make money. He wanted to know about investments, profits, contingencies and bad debts, all of which caused his teacher to consider him disruptive.

He saw school as a market to make money and so developed a small jewellery repair and stationery business (even selling to teachers) but was finally called to account by the Headmaster when he discovered a cache of over £300.00 in a locker. His father was called and the Headmaster explained the problem, asking what he was going to do about it. Scott's father responded by telling the Headmaster that rather than being angry, he was very proud of his son but was equally surprised that Scott had earned so little!

On leaving school at sixteen he found a job as an apprentice goldsmith where his chief mentor was an old jeweller called Jo who taught him to read people's mannerisms and look them in the eye. He learnt how to watch the actions of potential clients and recognise the 'buying' signs, i.e. when to push for or to drop the price to achieve a sale. He also gave Scott some advice that he has never forgotten: "there is no firm price for anything – it's what they're prepared to pay my son, it's what they're prepared to pay!"

At 17 he set up his own business – a jewellery repair operation. He employed other apprentices to do the work, paying them 50% of the income generated. He studied in the evening at the Cass Business School where he learnt that to make real money he needed to move into the world of corporate sales. At 20 he spotted a job opportunity to become a telecommunications salesman for the fledgling UK telecommunication company Mercury. The job interview required that he should be 21 years old, have a degree and live within the M25. He fulfilled none of these but turned up for the interview anyway as he knew he would be good at it. Despite their doubts and concerns, his sheer determination convinced them to give him a try. Almost reluctantly they employed him on a commission basis with no salary so that there was no risk to them in offering him the job. He was so successful that within 18 months he was the Sales Manager.

Despite his success and dramatic rise through the organisation, he felt somewhat constrained and believed that he could do better himself and so at age 21 he set up a new business called 'Network Europe Telecommunication' selling the latest 'smart-phone' technology. His first office was in a broom cupboard in the offices of one of his clients in Mayfair (in order to have a good address) and he employed his first salesman on a very high salary (for which he had to acquire guarantors) and for whom he provided a car, whilst he himself rode to work on a bicycle. All of this required not only extraordinary courage but critically, the confidence to believe that this process would work. He did not even have a set of accounts at this stage – just pure faith in his own abilities. Within two years his clients included the Banks of England and Canada and most of the Law Firms and Galleries in Central London.

The business was considered one of the 'rising stars' in telecoms in the UK, winning (in 1992) the award for the 'Most Dynamic Newcomer' in the telecoms Industry and later in 2004, the 'UK's Top Performing Dealership' award. He developed it into a highly effective operation and sold it at its peak. Interestingly over the years that followed he kept a close eye on the business, buying and selling the same company several times, finally splitting it into three divisions and selling the final part in 2011 to one of his competitors, Daisy Group Plc. (listed on the London Stock Exchange) for £26 million.

Scott has continued to expand his business interests over the years and has moved to Suffolk with his wife and four children, where his current main interest is the fast growing coffee business Paddy and Scott's, which he co-owns with Paddy Bishopp.

I put a number of questions to Scott to gain more of an insight into how he operates. His responses follow.

Q1. In setting up your first serious business you took a number of risks. You had no office, no money, no salesman and no vehicle. When you considered what to do, did you sit and listen to reason, or did you run with your gut feeling, your intuition?

It was a mixture of both. I reasoned that the product was excellent and would be easy to sell even to the largest of companies. My gut feeling (intuition) told me it felt right and continuously fed me with inspiring ways to make it work and thirdly, I trusted myself enough to take the risks necessary to get it started. It was certainly frightening but very exciting at the same time.

Q2. One of your first major breaks was your sale of the phone system to the Bank of England. The opportunity to do so presented itself in a most unusual way when you noticed that some BT engineers were making an awful racket outside their front door whilst laying a new cable. Tell us what happened and how you secured this really important deal?

Well I was walking past their offices and noticed all this work going on outside their front door and in that moment I had an intuitive flash of inspiration. So I walked in the front door and said how sorry I was about all the noise and was there anyone in particular I should speak to about it? I was ushered into the Operations Manager's office where I apologised for the noise outside and said that our company would be using that cable to host our services and that they need not worry about any further noise after it was completed. He was very pleased to hear this, accepted my apology and in the process I built a relationship with him. Bear in mind that the laying of the cable had absolutely nothing whatsoever to do with me! That was entirely a BT job. I then dropped in a word about our new phone systems and he put me in touch with the IT director.

That was the start of one of my most important business deals as once the Bank of England was operating one of our systems, it was an easy sell to others. The success of this deal was based on the fact that I acted on the intuition as it hit me and I had the balls to walk into the Bank of England with nothing more than a simple idea in the back of my mind.

Q3. The ego sustains most people but it can equally (and often does) become their worst enemy. In the pursuit of money, seemingly decent people are prepared to endorse actions that are 'damaging' to others and are clearly selfish. What is your philosophy in doing business, and does the same philosophy carry over into your private life?

My parents taught me that you should 'always treat people as you would wish to be treated' and that 'no-one wants to listen to your story' and that you have 'two ears and one mouth'; they said that these insights provided a good guideline for how I should conduct myself in my future life. I do think of these often and as a consequence I do treat people the way I would wish to be treated myself and I do not spend my time talking about my work. On the other hand if I am pitching my business, that is a whole different matter. I am very concentrated and focused when it comes to expanding the operation.

Equally, the ego often stops people from recognising that their business has failed. I have had a failed business and I am happy to admit it. The challenge is recognising when the business has actually failed and having the balls to stand up and say so. Many people continue to throw money at operations which are effectively dead using up important capital because they are not prepared to admit that the business has failed. Oddly, once I had admitted I had failed and I had set up a debt repayment plan, I was suddenly free to move on. The weight had lifted from me and I could move forward with a new vigour.

The sadness of course was that this affected all the employees of that company and that was not an easy challenge to deal with. Where possible we shifted people to the telecoms business but not everyone was right for that move.

I keep in contact with many of my previous employees and from time to time I have been able to assist some with challenging moments in their lives. I believe completely in ensuring that your workforce is well looked after and I have found that if I look after them, they will look after me. It fosters loyalty, and loyalty in business is very important.

Q4. Leadership is a very important part of running a successful business. How do you see your role as a leader in your operations?

If there are certain things I wish to achieve I generally plant the seed of an idea into someone's mind and I will nurture them and nudge them so that by the end of the meeting (or at least a short period of time) they have created the programme, they have developed a plan of action and indeed they have come up with an excellent remuneration package. The idea and the package is now theirs and they own it. I give them a 'high five' and I know that they will fly with the programme because it is now actually theirs, not mine. Often they go well beyond my initial ideas and so it really is their project.

I often make it clear that there is no such thing as a stupid idea, thus many interesting and unusual ideas fly around the table. Once again, if we consider these good and interesting and the figures add up, we nurture and encourage them until they come up with a solid plan themselves.

Q5. Whilst you have a very positive approach to your life and your business ventures, are your 'drivers' all positive?

As a kid I was told over and over again never to get into debt and to always pay my mortgage off. From time to time my parents would argue and I would hear comments like 'We'll end up living in a tent!' I loved my room and the idea of living in a freezing tent scared me so much that the fear has never gone away. I still wake up at night wondering if I have enough. It is like a primal fear; the tent looms and I wake up thinking 'what if, what if, what if....' so this fear is without doubt a key driver. Yes, I love the process of creating a successful business but without doubt I am also driven by this irrational fear of not having enough money to put food on the table or a roof over the heads of my family.

Q6. The success of your ventures has hinged not only on the ideas and products but very much on your ability to sell the product. Can you tell us something about that?

I work on the basis that if a person is willing to see me, then there is a need and they are interested in buying. Why else would they wish to see me unless they were simply wasting their time? I already know that I have a product that will fill their need. So, if they want to buy and I want to sell, what's the problem? Let's shake hands now and simply work out a deal. The barrier usually is the price, so once we have worked out a deal on the price, The last important question to ask is 'do you think we could work together and do you think I/we could manage the product for you?' If the answer is yes, then the deal is done. 'Sign here'. It really is so, so simple.

Let me give you an example. This coffee machine here (we are sitting in Paddy and Scott's head office in Suffolk) is built in Monaco for us. We help design the machine, how it works and how it can be integrated into our clients' businesses. This approach is unique. For example, if a client wants the machine wrapped in (say) Mulberry leather to create the concept of being highly upmarket, no problem, we'll get it done. We listen very carefully to their needs.

We were the first company to create branded phones in hotel bedrooms – when you picked the phone up in your room it would say 'Welcome Mr Russell' and the hospitality pad said 'Welcome, Mr Russell'. Now everybody has picked up on it and it is no longer a unique idea.

I see no point at all in 'the big sell', telling everyone how many years we have been in business and how wonderful our products are. People are generally tired of that and I find they are so relieved to have someone who is absolutely straight with them and indeed makes the whole process so simple and so easy. Selling is very simple.

Q7. The accepted business philosophy that 'for all things to move forward a clear goal should be determined' is very effective in that it gets things done. However, having a blueprint for the entire process seems to negate the possibility of any additional creative intervention. In other words in adopting the process, they sell themselves short. How do you feel about the concept of 'releasing the expectations of outcome'?

At the start of the financial year (for us November), we write a pretty in-depth business plan. It shows where we are going and how we intend to get there. We are only 6 months down the line and we are already on version 10 of the plan. It changes all the time. If we see a new opportunity and we do our due diligence, then we modify the plan to suit it. It drives my Managing Director nuts but it is critical; if one is to stay on top of the market, one must be open to new ideas. By remaining focused on one goal and one direction you miss the juicy fruit you could be grabbing on the way up.

Of course one cannot be frivolous especially with shareholder's money but if you remain blinkered to other opportunities, you really do miss out on the vast wealth of opportunity out there. Unfortunately most businesses do exactly this, thus limiting their potential for growth which is a terrible shame.

You only need to look at Aspall Cider to see a company who have kept their eyes open. Henry and Barry Chevallier Guild have taken it from a small local business to now having worldwide distribution and much diversification by keeping their eyes open and grabbing at new opportunities as they have emerged. I have the greatest respect for both of them.

Q8. One of the great concerns that people may have in making a decision to 'step out' and follow their heart is that they simply will not be able to finance themselves or their families or their way of life. You clearly made a decision to get on and make this work. If someone came to you asking for advice on what to do in order pursue their dreams, what would you say?

This is a very important question. In life, generally you don't regret things you do; you regret things that you don't do. If you have an idea and you don't pursue it, it will always be niggling in your mind, 'why didn't I do it?' If you are young and you have no ties or financial commitments, then my message would be, 'Do it! Just do it!'

If on the other hand you are married and/or perhaps have family, then there are other issues which you need to consider. You need to know how much your business will need in the first year and ensure you are covered for that and if that looks sound, then go for it. I have always had a contingency plan in place, not a great deal of money, but enough to sustain me if things did not work out as quickly as I have wanted them to. For example, I work on the basis that I need three months' worth of funds to cover the salary of a salesman. By the second month they are usually bringing in enough money to cover their income, so now I can look at a second salesman and so on and so on. Just make sure you have a contingency plan and go for it.

Coming up with a business concept is very simple really. For example, ask yourself how you would like to be treated when you walk into a hotel room. If you would like to be treated in a certain way, it is likely that others would too. Then you make a business out of how you would like best to be treated. Keep yourself open to new ideas. As Churchill once said, "Men occasionally stumble over the truth, but most of them pick themselves up and hurry off as if nothing has happened". The same is true of good business ideas. Be alert. They really are all around like fresh fruit, ready for the picking.

Conclusion

Scott is a straight talker. He doesn't beat around the bush and use flowery language; everything is very much to the point. Likewise, his business philosophy is very straight forward. One could argue that Scott is a very conventional businessman who has done well for himself through hard grit and common sense and of course this is correct. But there is more.

Scott recognises the value of his intuition. He is constantly open to new and inspiring ideas and 'listens' carefully when these ideas pop up. If they are worth considering and developing he will do so with zest. For him there is no such thing as a bad idea. Everything should be considered. It is of course the birthplace of original thought.

More than that, he understands that pinning your goals too firmly to the wall is not wise. As he points out, if you are not willing to look around and revisit your goals constantly, you will 'miss the juicy fruit' along the way. By releasing his fixation on the outcome he is allowing for change and the restructuring of his goals on a regular basis. This is clearly one of the reasons for his extraordinary success.

In 2011, Scott won the 'Suffolk Businessman of the Year' award, not only for the sale of his telecoms business but also as a result of the flourishing coffee business, Paddy and Scott's. Despite all the current economic challenges, this business is surging ahead whilst so many others are floundering.

So what else makes the difference?

Scott is comfortable with himself. Where some might have issues of doubt, Scott sees opportunity and takes it. If it fails, he makes every effort to work out why and moves on. Whilst he is very determined and very accomplished at what he does, he has not let all this success go to his head. He keeps well-grounded and is regularly at the rock face himself along with his staff. He enjoys the daily challenges and is not afraid to step into the unknown. Indeed, the unknown often offers extraordinary opportunity, some of which he has taken and continues to do so.

He remains an example to any inspired person seeking to move ahead in any direction. Listen to your intuition, do your due diligence, allow for adjustments and 'have the balls' to step out. I am sure he will still be at the rock face for many years to come.

Visit **www.cultivating-intuition.com** *for more background, links to talks, images, references and a regular blog of new ideas.*

16

Francois Le Roux - the 'HA!Man'™

An intuitive musician who inspires others to recognise the music within them

Francois Le Roux in action

Francois Le Roux is a musician with a difference. Whilst he has played music since he was a child and has trained as a classical cellist, he chooses not to try and perfect his ability as a classical player. Rather, he prefers the raw quality of spontaneous music. This is where, for him, the real engagement with life exists. It is raw, it is intuitive and it is played as a very direct response to the atmosphere and energy that surrounds the player at the time. It is not simply playing – it is BEING.

Francois was born in 1966 to an Afrikaans preacher and his music teacher wife on the goldfields of South Africa. He had a natural desire to play music and has been improvising since the age of four. At age ten he was appointed church organist and at eleven performed for the first time as solo cellist with an orchestra. His formative years were further marked by a series of compositions and musical awards but also chess, rugby, handiwork, scout leadership and church activities. His formal musical training started with his mother and stretched into his early twenties, when he decided to focus primarily on spontaneous music making.

South Africa was still in the throes of Apartheid and he was called to do two years military service as an artilleryman. Afterwards, love drew him towards Stellenbosch to study theology in the footsteps of his father. This was not an easy time. The years 1986-88 marked a deep inner shift as he simultaneously grappled with the meaning of faith, the dualistic tendencies of western thought and the state of emergency in South Africa.

Halfway through his theology degree he hit an existential dead end. Neither his faith and philosophy nor his musical heritage sustained him in a viable manner anymore. Estranged from his past and society, he returned to the birth of his interest in music and took to the stage with fully improvised recitals. From 1992-2000 he hitch-hiked throughout South Africa, busking on streets, performing in houses, writing, drawing and dancing.

He continued to learn the cello and under the tutelage of Dalena Roux, he discovered the way in which expression actually starts with the body and how feeling can deconstruct the mind. This journey was amplified by the political stage, where he witnessed first-hand how the raw human energy of Africa put cracks all over a de-humanizing ideological system. As he pitched his tent in wild places his awareness deepened: how the body of humanity for ages had systemized the earth and strained natural organic rhythms. He changed his diet towards raw fruits and sprouts. These experiences and the sustained health he has since enjoyed have helped to change his view of his role as a musician and performer.

The more he played, the more he was encouraged by others to seek greater exposure and potential fame. He found himself sharing the stage with some of the world's top performers but always shied away from following this route. His concern has always been that in turning professional he would have to conform more to the requirements of the organisers of these events and thus the shows would become less spontaneous and that it would take him far from his home in South Africa. His performances and workshops are different and the organisers and managers of the musical world would find him difficult to put into a specific category – he does not fit into a precise and easily explainable pigeonhole and thus they would seek to manipulate him into a 'manageable' box. He does however travel and play across the USA and in Europe but it is always on his own terms.

Francois particularly enjoys working with young people and especially pre-teenage children as their eagerness, their freedom from inhibitions and their exuberance fuels his own creativity and energy.

In a biographical piece published on his website recently, the writer asked the following question:

"The intense challenge remains for any exceptional talent like his to at once survive to make its mark as well as to facilitate true empowerment. Is he perhaps creating a legacy of one, who, in this age of 'endless' growth and rapid expansion, tries (through his gift of music and expression) to reconnect the dots between a deep, mysterious past and an uncertain future, questioning both our material and spiritual gods in order to touch on something that could be called human maturity?"

The interview below answers some of these questions. Francois has made a conscious choice to follow the route he is on and his decision is rooted in his own deep personal understanding of the meaning and purpose of life. His answers are extremely thought provoking and very revealing of the challenges he has had to face in taking the decision to follow his heart.

Q1. You have written about your 'deep inner shift' between 1986 and 1988 and your subsequent 'estrangement' from your past and from society in South Africa. This must have been a deeply challenging time when you were really not certain of who you were or what you were doing, although you seemed to know clearly that you wished to be a musician. It strikes me that this must have been a period of great vulnerability for you. You had broken the 'norms' of accepted behaviour and whilst you had made the choice to do this, you must have been ridden with doubt from time to time. How did you cope during this very challenging period?

At first I was hiding it all inside. I was at the time a student at Stellenbosch University, studying to become a minister in the church. I was really losing my stability in believing in a personal god. The faith complex within me faded, was strengthened anew, to just fade again. Cycles of doubt and anxiety and new insights. It amazed me how, through the creative application of language (supported by the Bible), I could still have a meaningful life within the church, even as a leader, without revealing my deepest doubts. As the faith structure slowly crumbled, it made way for a closer relationship to my body for instance. This in turn liberated my mind and senses so that the world could be seen and experienced in new and more open ways. This was seen and felt by others and often interpreted as spiritual growth. It would all depend on how far I could walk this road of new enlightenment (and darkness) and still be accepted within the faith community. Thus, I 'coped' by virtue of the fact that doubt is only one side of the coin. Doubt prepares the ground for new insights and as long as those can be meaningfully shared, one is saved from becoming alienated. I also coped by keeping conversations alive with those who had a sympathy and some understanding for my journey. Even though I often felt that such conversational friends did not fully grasp all my questions, conversing serves as a channel for emotional sharing, and that flow of feeling contributes to keep one's sanity intact.

But then again, I also did NOT cope. I often broke down emotionally, taking flight with my bicycle into the mountains. Some relationships broke off, including my first serious love. A deep darkness grew inside of me as I began to realise that I would not ultimately be able to remain within the embrace of the faith community I grew up in. Communications with my mother (my father died when I was seven) also became very strained and convulsive. I was losing my anchors and the only way to cope with that was to consolidate, economize, digging deeper to find possible seeds for a small and new beginning.

I was able to finish my degree and church activities without breaking down completely. I switched my studies to music and found a room on a farm to stay in. A new relationship developed with a rebellious woman older than me. Some loose links remained with the church, but for all practical purposes I was out. I then threw myself completely into the world of music.

Q2. Having seen one of your workshops and been so affected by not only the music but also the effect it had on all the participants and indeed on all those watching, it seems to me that what you are doing is opening a doorway to their intuition and 'giving them permission' to break with conventional teachings and 'norms' and allow themselves to 'taste' their own extraordinary natural creativity. How do you feel about this analogy? How does your thought process work in the act of conducting one of your performances or workshops?

The analogy is apt, albeit only from a more objective point of view. Conducting such a workshop, however, does not proceed from any conscious aim to break norms or make people discover themselves. Often such aims only succeed in creating yet another norm or rule that prevents the surprise of true discovery. The reality is also of course that no such liberation is guaranteed and even if a breakthrough is made it might not be a pleasant experience, nor one that has any lasting effect.

I call myself the "HA!" man exactly because I lack a rational basis for what I do. "HA!" is not a rational concept. It is an expression, but an expression of what? It can certainly convey something, but that something is never fixed. Nor can it be taken for granted that it will be meaningful. And this is where the vulnerability sets in: nothing that can be held by the conscious mind can serve as an anchor in this process. I enter in silence. I proceed from an animal-like state, a pre-conscious state (that corresponds to a prehistorical or child-like state) and I most often use no words until well into the process.

I cannot lead participants towards an outcome. I can only BE, and through being, facilitate an environment that may be of expansionary value for those present. So if you ask me about thought processes, I can only confess that thought processes in themselves are counter-productive, unless you include under the umbrella of 'process' mental events like paradoxical thinking and meditative states - both of which serve to counteract a dominant mind so that feeling can flow through.

The question should rather be 'how to describe the state of being you are in while you conduct such a workshop?' Then I would refer to three basic aspects of being, all of which play a role in the process: the instinctive, the mental and the emotive. On a gut or instinctive level, silences and raw physical power emanate. On a mental level, meaning is expressed in metaphorical and often paradoxical ways like, "if you'd like to express yourself freely then be totally focused" or, "become a fountain" or, "do not do anything until you feel wet." Finally, on the emotive level (which forms the crux of the whole event), feeling myself, the surrounding atmosphere, the whole group and each participant. Therein lies the deeper art, a dialogue of sensitivities, a play with colour, an openness to be human with each other.

It is in this sprouting of a certain state of being that the creative moment can occur on either a raw or an experienced level. And when it occurs, even that cannot be taken for granted or be properly defined. Nor can it be captured in order to be repeated. Most often, rational approaches to creativity try to capture that 'which works' so that this can be outlined for repeated use. Even the most sublime moment of artistic expression has its natural ending and needs to leave space for the next unknown.

The conclusion is not an outcome nor a product but an event that lived with the fullness of flow.

Q3. You mention that working in education and with young people is given special focus. What is it about working with young people that is so inspiring for you? What is it that you are trying to convey to them?

The most obvious answer is that being young naturally leaves more scope for spontaneous expression, as life is still largely unformed and free from too many constraints of surviving and succeeding in society. Secondly, creativity in itself is a youthful exercise as it makes itself busy with that which is new and fresh. Given this, it is a natural choice for me to work with younger people. There's a mutual attraction at work here.

It does not close the door to working with other age groups too, of course. Creativity in that sense knows no boundaries. A good friend of mine who is turning 100 years old this year has this as one of his mottos: that to live a lasting life one needs to remain creative all along - something that he has achieved to a remarkable degree.

What I do get back from young people is their raw energies. They give me the freedom to be far more playful on stage than is possible with adult audiences. And I think that my regular performances are emboldened by spending good amounts of time with younger people and especially pre-teenage children.

Again, the question of 'conveying' something to them is not quite apt, as I hardly have any 'message' in mind. I do exude a certain energy and my primary responsibility to them is to be myself in a most creative way, rather than to deliver a message or 'things to remember.' I believe that the meaning that is 'left behind' (and is reflected in the many outpourings of excitement, even life-changing experiences) springs mainly from what happens between us, rather than that which passed from me to them. Yes of course, I do enter with a certain focus and specialized experience, but all that is rather lame without that which is coming back from them, including their own creative beings. If change or the breakdown of constrictive norms is what is to be achieved, that comes about more effectively by acting-from-within by all who are present, rather than from a one-way process of conveying.

Q4. Entertaining and performing appear to come easy for you and yet your performances are not choreographed affairs. When I saw you run the workshop in Zimbabwe it was a spontaneous event and it was that factor that gave it its magic. However this approach is in conflict with an accepted business philosophy that 'for all things to move forward effectively, a clear structure and goal should be determined'. It is of course a very effective method in that it gets things done, but having a blueprint for the entire process seems to negate the possibility of any additional creative intervention. In other words in adopting the process, they sell themselves short. As an artist, how do you feel about the concept of 'releasing the expectations of outcome'?

I have already touched upon this. I think working towards the future is a devil. Yet it is a hallmark of human consciousness probably since the dawn of civilization. We have smartly developed linear structures in our minds, indeed to 'get things done' and make survival of a species possible on a scale never seen before on this planet. Yet working towards goals all rests on a fundamental illusion and that illusion is that the future is attainable at all. We do not walk our lives on a line from the past through the present until the end of the future. We always remain in the present. In fact, if we were able to reach the future it would lose its meaning. The very essence of the future is that it is more open and unknown, just like a far-off horizon is to the traveller. Once that horizon is reached it is no horizon anymore. Behold! Another horizon lies ahead. It is only in our minds that we can sustain the illusion that 'one day we will reach the future.'

Indeed, there is no magic in working towards a future goal. It sucks us dry from being surprised and it makes us fearful of discovery. Working towards a goal is an effort to narrow reality down to more elementary elements that can more easily be manipulated. But we are paying a huge price in the process. We lose balance. We keep on leaning forward. We lose the fullness of living in the present and we neglect our past - that which should form a counterweight to the future. The result is not what we wish it to be, i.e. being more effective and economical. The deeper result is that we are never satisfied because we believe in reaching something that can never be reached. And so we created a world that forever dreams about and is planning to fix things for the future. Yet all along the way it creates such a web of complexities and intractable problems just because we fail to reckon with the whole. And the whole lies in and all around us. Not just in front of us.

I could enter a workshop with the idea that I want to inspire kids to become musicians. Or I could enter it making music and by chance infect those present to make music too. In the first case, I shape my work to serve the future. In the second, I work as a matter of present interest. In the first, I present. In the second, I am present. The first might just put a few kids on a trajectory to become pianists, singers and band players. The second makes musicians of all for that moment. In which scenario were things really getting done?

It is a deep question, pertaining to all aspects of society. In the economy for instance, do we 'grow it' in order to 'create wealth?' Or do we look at that which is at hand and sustainably accessible and economize our material lives around it?

The trick is that the musician who lives with the future in mind plays and looks differently from the one who plays with spontaneous expression and these two are often cast in opposition to each other. The future-focused musician specializes and achieves abnormal levels of skill that impresses others into a humble silence. The organic musician who just makes music, however raw and unpolished it might be, who experiences growth as a side-effect and not as a conscious goal, that musician is the one that can deliver magic with simple means and who might also impress, though not necessarily humbling others. The first adds music onto life, the second uses it as an expression of life. The first carries music with great effort and commitment, the second breathes it. The first's fulfilment lies in the glorious moments of achievement, the second's fulfilment lies in being music each time it is expressed and can be carried through until its last breath.

If by 'releasing the expectations of outcome' you mean that those expectations should be relaxed, I would again put it in paradoxical terms: the outcome that lives in you as a longing can only be achieved when it is forgotten. Being on stage often means to me to take those very real desires (of technical mastery of an instrument for instance) not as an outcome, but as a bundle of energy that can be invested in the present moment. Therefore, the conscious desire is brought into the whole, rather than projected away onto an abstract timeline. The result is mostly that the outcomes do appear eventually, yet the primary experience and focus is not that of achievement, but that of continuous fulfilment, with so many more aspects coming into play than just the future.

It is in this sense that much more is getting done than when you narrow your scope in order to take a shortcut. Our future-obsessed culture gets things done indeed, but pretty much only on a surface level. It all shines well, yet leaves layers and layers underneath in a neglected state. And then we wonder why we are afflicted with cancers, environmental doom and all sorts of depression?

Yet on this world-view stage I can also just BE, rather than provide directives as to how to operate with a presence-consciousness as a business for instance. As an artist I can only

BE that consciousness within my limited means, throwing seeds to the unknown. Healing, like the magic you describe, is no achievement.

Q5. You have obviously had to work hard to develop your 'work base' over the years with a lot of effort on your part networking amongst friends and admirers across the world. There must however have been moments when you wondered where the money to buy your next meal would come from?

One of the great concerns that people may have in making a decision to 'step out' and follow their own hearts is that they simply will not be able to finance themselves or their families or their way of life. You clearly made a decision to get on and make this work, despite the concerns that you would have to earn a living. How have you coped with this and what would your advice be to someone considering 'stepping out'?

There is a very simple, yet serious realization that came over me through the years. And that is that money does not make people. People make money. Put in another way, money was not first, people were first. There can be people without money, but no money without people.

There is actually quite a strong parallel between the future and money. Both are abstractions. And both are made into gods that we choose to serve. 'Living for the future' or 'Live to earn money' are both expressing the desire to narrow life towards means that can be manipulated more easily. If I have money, I can buy all this stuff. It gives me power. Or if I have a clear goal, I can order my life effectively and remove doubts and grey areas. But again the illusion: just as the future cannot be reached as it always remains secondary to the present, just so can money never deliver the power it promises, because money derives its very meaning from people and not the other way around.

Yes, money has been a big theme all along my path as an improviser. I was often told how I could apply my talents better in order to earn more (become more famous). Yet I have never been out of money, except once when I had to ask a friend for about 20 pounds just to get by (a friend who offered to help me anytime I really hit the wall). Through the years of hitch-hiking in South Africa my overheads were minimal. I never lacked. But after buying a car and computer and building amplified music sets on three continents, my overheads rapidly rose and I was vulnerable to robberies, constant maintenance costs and especially transport costs. I often had fantasies of riches and fame and was rather open to being taken up in the more mainstream arenas, yet, always stopping short of giving up on my core focus of spontaneous (present-orientated) music making. Currently, after 20 years, I am doing financially just well enough to survive in a healthy way.

The reality is that in order to make this shift (towards a life and living that is deeply connected to my core being) I did go to lengths that most people would probably shy away from. For a decade I had no vehicle, hitch-hiking my way with a backpack on my back - which contained all my material possessions. I broke almost every rule in the book of modern day survival. I did not ask myself 'what do the people want.' I did not research where my 'niche-market' would lie. I did not insure myself. I did not try to make money out of money. I did not go after sponsors or grants. I definitely did not have a 'steady income' as an ideal.

So what did I develop then? How did I secure survival in a money-obsessed world? I can only say that I did three things. I asked myself: what do I want to do? And answered (the answer took years to reach me) that I want to go on stage with nothing. Then I asked myself: what is my success as an artist? My answer very early on was this: people. In relating to people, connecting, networking and communicating, in the exchange of meaning. This I saw as the very basis of my 'career' - my insurance, my joy and my inspiration. Thirdly, I applied myself to these two things and all that it implies and entails: spontaneous performance and relating to people - audiences, hosts, friends, supporters and strangers. Thus, my life consists mainly of performing and communicating and then moving along these life-posts of stages and people connections. And just like the future becomes a side-effect of the fulfilment of the present, so money becomes a side-effect of performing and relating to people.

I cannot give any specific advice. I can only be witness to the act that living from the primary elements mostly takes care of the secondary. Money is a devil too. We simply should not allow it to blind us to the fact that we created it in the first place.

Q6. You have alluded to the fact that you have often played with well-known people in important locations and the opportunity has been there for you to move country and step out and become a respected world recognised musician. Yet you have chosen to stay close to your roots and the continent from which you came. There is obviously a driving force behind this decision. With the potential of fame and international recognition there for you, what is it that keeps you from taking that step?

How much I have the potential - as an improvising musician - to become a known player on the world stage is a moot question. It actually begs the question in what way can the vulnerability of spontaneous performance survive the cranked-up lime lights of our global culture?

The added question should be why did I not then choose to shape my art into a more sellable commodity? And furthermore, is it really a requirement to be based abroad in order to become world-recognized?

I have never closed the door to entering more illustrious avenues as such, and there were many such encounters through the years. But even as I pursued these, they mostly reached dead-ends that I can mainly ascribe to at least two factors: they usually demand a higher level of specialization (especially in order to be able to 'box' you into a more recognizable category) and they had to compete with a rhythm that I have already grown with patterns of touring and voluntary commitments to people and places around the world. I therefore hardly ever found myself in a begging position and I gradually gained more and more confidence to say: *"well, if you would like to have me, take me for what I have become. Otherwise, peace!"*

Often people would be very taken by my work and would feel frustrated that I am not known much more widely. They then wish me to find my 'big break' somewhere along the line, or they would reprimand me for not promoting myself properly, or letting myself be promoted properly.

Perhaps I should put my position regards these comments in negative terms: that yes, it is my fault that I find constant high levels of fulfilment, whether I play to 10 or 1000 people, whether in a location of no consequence or in one of note. I therefore lack the inner drive to climb the ladder so to speak. I am a weak achiever.

But I have made my peace in this regard. Working spontaneously is really digging into a more original field of music making and as such it is more about planting seeds than tending orchards full of fruit for masses of people to eat. And working with seeds asks for its own kind of input and nourishment. I therefore certainly find more nourishment in the continent of origins (Africa) than in a northern one where spaces are cramped out with orchards and lots of human fruits.

I do believe that there is still much scope for my contribution to be made effective on a wider scale, even if simply by natural growth as I move on in my (more primitive) way. Yet at the same time I am aware that I choose to work on a level that is not exactly conducive to mass consumption. Again, if I have to be recognized more widely, let this sprout from where I am based. And if I ever have to shift base, it must be for far more reasons than just to add quantity and fame to my name - both of which carries problems and limitations of their own.

Besides, I truly love (South) Africa and am glad to be able to call it home.

17

Joanna Jones – an artist with a difference

Joanna Jones: photo by Caspar Krabo

Joanna Jones is a highly accomplished and well respected British painter who lives in Dover. Her work and how she paints it is both fascinating and absorbing as it is very different to any other artist I know of. It is unique.

Joanna studied art at Northwich College of Art, the Byam Shaw School, Goldsmiths College and finally the Royal Academy Schools in London, finishing her 'structured' education in 1970.

During her final years at the Royal Academy Schools, she had begun to move away from painting in its traditional sense as she found it increasingly difficult to know what to paint; the subject matter became less important than the act of painting itself. She began searching for a new way of expressing her art and turned towards performance; and through performance, she found a

171

dynamic new way of expressing herself - she became the piece of art itself. It seemed more 'real' than a painting, a direct 'experience' of life. Without her full physical and mental participation, there was no piece of art to show.

It was the direct physicality, the act of being 'inside' the art itself that she found so inspiring, so energising. It was a very exciting period in her life and she moved to Frankfurt in Germany to be in an environment of 'progressiveness' and vitality. Frankfurt was at the time at the heart of a renaissance in the German art scene.

Performance dominated her artistic output for a while but Joanna really missed her work with paint. She loved painting and was, by nature, a colourist. She ached for a way of being able to integrate her performance with painting as the two methods of expression seemed so far apart. She listened to her intuition and slowly, slowly she began a process of bringing the two processes together. At first they were just experiments, but more and more she realised that the act of making marks with her body on the canvas, the more she felt a part of the painting itself. Not only was she the painter, she was physically connected to the canvas – and what was left on the canvas at the end was the beautiful 'residue' of an intense experience derived from a blend of intuition and creativity, the result being a truly original piece of work.

In an interview with Guy Brett (a much published Art Historian) in 2005, Joanna was able to describe aspects of her work which clarify what she was/is aiming to achieve.

"*What prompted me the first time to this act was an overwhelming wish to enter my painting and do away with any separation between my work and myself...This way of working directly with my own being – my own vibration in the act of painting – is the way I have worked since 1983. I paint through touch and not through sight. It is not my hands that I use but my whole body – which means I cannot see. I can only feel what I am doing for the duration of the act. Each time I enter a work I privilege my tactile sense over my visual sense. This process generates forms, textures and fine structures that it would not be possible to create in any other way.*

These 'body strokes' are always different. I find them sensual, some extremely beautiful; others uncanny, some almost grotesque or they can be all of these at different times or shifting in the process of looking. The results of an action are always unexpected and can bring about compositions I could never have imagined. I have kept the aspects of performance that I so value and have brought them to my painting practice but I do this privately in my studio and present the final paintings publicly."

"My interest is in being, in energy and the nature of thought and matter. The act of painting is the moment of action when the mind and body are given over to something outside of mental or visual control expressing through movement, perhaps tactile memory, in that sublime moment in contact with the paint. I work with an active female body; my work celebrates the vital body and seeks to address the neglect and repression that occurs when the body is reduced to its external form."

"At first it was all very difficult but gradually as I began to find the right consistency for the paint as well as a suitable smoothness for the ground of the canvas, forms emerged out of the action that reminded me of cloths with a life of their own. It was interesting that my wish to give form to my own vitality directly with my own body would create forms that resemble those that artists have been using through centuries connected with the human being, perhaps to express a similar content."

As a consequence of applying marks in this way, the painting can go through a remarkable adjustment in just one application of paint, completely changing the whole perception of the painting. Joanna thus spends a great deal of time as the viewer of her own work, absorbing the visual imagery and coming to terms with what stands in front of her. This then becomes the starting point for her next application of paint (or not as the case may be).

An area that particularly fascinates Joanna is how viewers respond to her work.

"One point that I should like to make about viewing my work is that

I think one has to actually stand before a painting of mine to really feel it. The painting and the viewer are related in scale and energy; if viewed in reproduction this is missing. The viewer who is prepared to let down their guard and enter the visual world I have created seems to travel tactilely with their eyes through the painting, connecting with it on an energetic level...often the viewer is making associations and looking for references. There is also the feeling that the forms are somehow recognisable."

"What is very interesting is that I have never had anyone know, without being told, that the forms are made with the human body. They make associations with cloud formation, exotic vegetation, billowing cloth, internal organs but never the human body as we see it. There are then the references to art history and artists that people are reminded of such as Turner or Blake, Tiepolo or Grünewald. From these associations one can see an aspect of how the effect of the inner light of the paintings is affecting the viewer. There follows then often an uncomfortable-ness and irritation.... "What are these works?" Eventually when the viewer has exhausted their possibilities of association and reference and given up trying to solve the puzzle they either disengage from the process of looking and move on or they start to physically engage with the work."

"It is very different when the viewer knows that the paintings are painted with the body. Then there is a tendency to look for body parts. "Is that your arm? Did you do that with your...?" I try to explain that I use my body to move the paint. That they will find no direct print of a body part since I am in movement when I am painting, using the body to spread the paint. There is also often a feeling that, because I use my body, the paintings happen automatically without my having any part in the painting's creation."

After the death of her husband in 2002, Joanna was so deeply affected that she was unable to produce any work for some time. *"I found myself unable to enter the fullness of the physicality of my work; actually I couldn't bear the feel of the paint on my skin."*

During this period, working closely with a friend and fellow artist Clare Smith, Joanna decided to throw her energy into something completely different. It was a way of embracing the change in her life and has turned out to be an extraordinarily successful venture.

Joanna and Clare decided to form a company called the 'Dover Arts Development' (DAD) to develop a programme of contemporary visual art in Dover and link into the emerging art landscape of the South East. They have now been developing projects since 2006. Funding is sought for each new project so it takes a fair amount of effort and determination to ensure a project is completed. They recently completed a 90 minute feature documentary film 'Watermark' about the paper mill (formerly the producers of Conqueror paper and closed in 2000) told through the stories of the men and women who worked there.

"The genesis of "Watermark" was a DVD put into my handbag by one former employee who didn't want to be interviewed showing the last paper run at Buckland Mill. In the end we involved over 300 former employees in the film. We presented 50 hours of in depth oral histories to Dover Museum and the University of Kent for further research. We have reunited a traumatised paper making community many of whose families have been in Dover making paper for over 300 years and also found a way to tell their story which is also a more general story of deindustrialisation, the advance of technology and the ensuing change to a former industrial town."

Joanna and Clare work out of their homes. They have no 'centre' as such. When projects are underway, Joanna often houses visiting artists or producers. "When artists are staying we cook together in the evening and hospitality has become an important part of the DAD ethos with artist dinners and salons around food as an important part of our activities."

I put a number of questions to Joanna in order to try and understand, over and above what I had already read, exactly what drives her forward.

Q1. Coming up with the idea to paint with your body initially and making your first few attempts must have been very exciting and inspiring on the one hand but there must have been serious moments of doubt. External concerns of 'what will others think of it? Will they think I am crazy? Will they think this is weird?' What was it that kept you going through this period?

I was living in Germany at the time. I had known for a long time that I wanted to get back to painting but I just didn't know how. I couldn't speak the German language very well and this frustration and a longing to find a way to involve my whole being led to this step. I wanted to express something about being alive by being alive.

I was living in Frankfurt which has a history of 'free thinking'. It was 1983; the artists and those interested in art were open at that time. With Germany's recent past, no one wanted to be seen as restrictive to new ideas. Also, having not studied there and knowing few people, I was effectively anonymous.

If I had stayed in England I doubt that I would have taken this step. My own mother once said to me that she was glad she could not read German to read what was being said about my 'dirty' way of working. That was quite a shock.

And I did have my boyfriend of 5 years walk out saying if people could make a living from moving around in paint on a canvas then the whole world would be rich.

To be honest there are times when I wonder why I set out to do something so difficult but on the other hand when a work comes through and is beautiful and free and others are able to engage with it, then that is the most wonderful feeling in the world.

Q2. Many artists, particularly since Piero della Francesca have used geometry and the golden section to carefully work out the structures of their paintings. Thus a huge amount of work went into the planning of the picture even before a single drop of paint was applied to the canvas - a lot of mental processing. In your work, this whole process appears to be reversed as you are making one mark followed by another mark and building the picture based on your responses to the marks that have previously been made. In other words, there is no plan. Thus the 'balance' in the pictures tends to appear later on. It seems to me therefore that your intuition plays a large part in this process. The golden section appears in so many of the natural things around us (for example, the structure of the human face) and is thus a part of nature's 'natural' design. It thus seems logical to me that it is a blend of your intuition guiding you and your application of thought to that inspiration that causes these extraordinary paintings to emerge as they do. How do you feel about this analogy? How does your thought process work in the making of one of your paintings?

You have expressed the process very well. As I work from the premise that everything is interrelated it would follow that naturally forms of balance sometimes exactly following the golden section will be formed. My body is one such form and in its movement it will always move within its natural possibilities. I have to be constantly vigilant though and it feels like tight rope walking, staying true to the spark of intuition and not allowing my lower mind to attempt control out of fear. I aspire to let my intuitive mind lead the whole building of the work as well as each individual action. It requires real attention to the moment, a stilling of the mind, the action coming from a place of real vulnerability.

Q3. In your email conversation with Guy Brett in 2005, you said the following: "I paint through touch and not through sight. It is not my hands that I use but my whole body – which means I cannot see. I can only feel what I am doing for the duration of the act. Each time I enter a work I privilege my tactile sense over my visual sense... The act of painting is the moment of action when the mind and body are given over to something outside of mental or visual control expressing through movement." It seems to me that, more than most artists you are engaging your entire self, indeed all your senses in the process of making the art. There is certainly the tactile aspect of the body moving the paint on the canvas, but has every move been planned once you begin? You will have built up some ideas in

177

your mind already (hence the colours applied and the starting point for your next application), but do you allow your senses to guide you once you are actually applying the paint? Do you 'feel' into the energy of the picture and allow it to guide you in the application process?

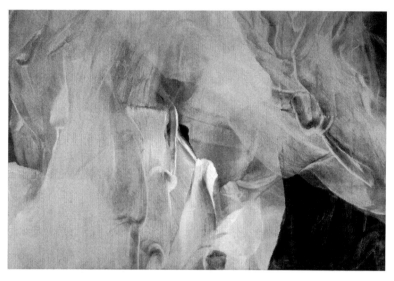

"Where did that come from?" by Joanna Jones - 1999

I have NO idea of the final composition though I am a colourist. I mix my own paint from raw pigment with the yolk of an egg – and I mix a fluid egg tempera. I use my knowledge of colour, how certain colours will react over other colours and the different properties of opaqueness and transparency of different pigments. It is so difficult to explain what happens once I have made contact with the paint and am about to spread it. My body moves how it likes and can. By 'can', I mean I cannot move where there is no paint. The wet paint allows me to make a movement but it is impossible for me to know what the result of that action will look like or how it responded and relates to the previous action or actions.

Q4. The accepted business philosophy that 'for all things to move forward a clear goal should be determined' is very effective in that it gets things done. However, having a blueprint for the entire process seems to negate the possibility of any additional creative intervention. In other words in adopting the process, they sell themselves short. As an artist, how do you feel about the concept of 'releasing the expectations of outcome'?

That is key to my process of making and key to the intrinsic power of a work. It is also key to my process of living.

The process I try to adopt at each stage within a work is to release every expectation of outcome once the colour, paint mixture and position of where I pour the first 'puddle' of paint and allow the body to create the form it moves into creating in that moment. Once I stand back from the canvas to view what I have created I also have to allow it to be. Quite often I have thought that I didn't like something just because I had not come to know it, so there too I have to be careful and as sure as I can be where the impulse to take the possibility to change a form is coming from: is it from fear and anxiety or is it, as sometimes, because I have missed a lot of paint or the action has been interrupted in some way in which case I have a few minutes to move the paint again before the paint begins to dry. I have about 7 minutes for that decision

Q5. You have been one of the key people in the setting up of the Dover Arts Development (DAD) project. This now takes up a lot of your time. What is it about your work with the project and the resulting activity that drives you on to do more? Does this have a connection with your need to be 'inside' one of your paintings whilst you are working on it?

The way our projects develop is so similar to making a painting. It is attention to detail, never losing sight of the big picture but never thinking one knows how things are going to develop. Staying alert, taking opportunities as they arise and staying adaptive and flexible if something is not working. DAD is alive and exciting because we don't know what is going to happen next.

I am now painting again and with DAD I have created a way of life that I once again feel comfortable within. Again it has to do with embodiment and connection. I guess this is my need to be 'inside' a work that you so intuitively picked up.

Q6. One of the great concerns that people may have in making a decision to 'step out' and follow their heart is that they simply will not be able to finance themselves or their families or their way of life. You clearly made a decision to get on and make this work, despite the concerns that you would have to earn a living. How have you coped with this? Has there been a corresponding mental approach to how you have lived your life, which has clearly evolved, as all of our lives do?

It is hard and I have had my share of stomach cramps not knowing where the next money is coming from. I have done all sorts of different things during tough financial times but I have also been very lucky. What I can now see is that if you spend your time doing what fulfils you, you will be happy to live relatively simply because the riches will be in what you do, who you meet and how you feel. The need to make more money than you need for reasonable comfort seems to be a substitute for really being alive

If you are in tune with yourself doing what you are called to do with your life then you find yourself full of energy and that energy will take you forward. Doubt does come in and some moves really do seem like mistakes but everything leads on to the next stage and develops from where it was; and throughout it all you are living your life, alive and awake.

Q7. If someone came to you asking for advice on what to do in order to pursue their dreams, what would you say?

I should try to help them see that if they already have a dream then they have started their journey and the way continues, one step at a time.

Conclusion

Joanna's life has been driven by a desire to create, a desire to express herself in the best way possible. She has been through some difficult times; even faced her mother's harsh criticism and her boyfriend's rejection as a result of her work and that cannot have been easy, as when the 'cut' comes from someone very close it can be deeply hurtful. Yet she has stayed consistent with her dreams. As she says, some moves do seem like mistakes but in the long run they are simply a part of the journey and when a painting comes together and really works powerfully, there is no greater feeling of satisfaction in the world.

Joanna remains full of energy and vitality. She lives life richly and directly and there is no doubt that she has a great deal more still to accomplish.

At the end of the first paragraph at the start of this chapter, I described Joanna's work as unique. It is and delightfully so, but the lesson to be learnt here is that all of us are unique individuals and thus we all have unique potentials. Grasping the nettle, trusting your intuition and allowing yourself to develop and cultivate ideas and follow them through will allow you also to create unique work of your own, whatever it may be. As Joanna points out above, if you already have a dream you have already started your journey; keep walking.

18

Becky Overy-Owen - Flying high after the fall

Becky Overy Owen

Becky was born in 1971, the youngest of five children and by five years. Her father was a highly successful businessman who focused pretty exclusively on his business, a large pig farm. At that time, farming was considered a lifestyle choice rather than a profitable enterprise. He sought to change that and by the time he died, he had created the largest privately owned farming business in the country.

He was a surprisingly unemotional man and was never really at home. He would take her swimming from time to time but it was never a casual swim; it was always about how much better she could become. She learnt early that if she wanted his 'love', she needed to achieve, to meet his expectations. If he was ever disappointed, he simply said nothing at all. When her school reports came in, she used to sit, afraid, awaiting his response which, owing to low grades, was generally one of silence. The silence was always deafening.

As a consequence, she felt inadequate and developed a very low self-esteem. Later at boarding school (which she quite enjoyed as the atmosphere at home was often tense) she recalled the annual father/daughter tennis matches. She was an accomplished tennis player for her age but the moment her father stepped onto the court with her, so desperate was she to please him that she would go to pieces and mess everything up. He would say nothing (which made it worse) and wander off whilst she would put on a brave face, feeling quite useless and pathetic.

Her mother was very protective of her (herself the youngest of five), though she was going through her own severe problems. She was very unhappy in her marriage and had an eating disorder (bulimia) which affected her a lot of the time and she was often 'unwell' in her room. Becky remembered that there was a lot of 'confusion' over quite what was 'going on' with her mother. Her parents separated when she was 11 and she and her second sister went to live with her mother whilst her brother stayed with her father. The elder siblings had already left home.

Similarly, Becky began to develop her own eating disorders (anorexia and bulimia) when she was 16 which, she reflects now, was a way of trying to control her own emotions which were painful and confused and which had not really been nurtured very well as she had grown up. She also recognises now that addictive behaviour was very much a part of both her mother's and her father's lives (he was a workaholic and an exercise fanatic) so she believes it was already part of her own makeup.

She completed 2 'A' levels and set off on a truly amazing gap year overland across Asia which she remembers with great fondness and looks back on now, drawing inspiration from the fun and confidence she enjoyed over that period. She felt in control of her anorexic behaviour and although she had begun to drink more, that too was under control.

Soon after her return she went into training as a nurse which, whilst gratifying, she found somewhat challenging to her emotions and found it difficult to switch off from the pain and stress of the day. As a result she began drinking more heavily to ease the anxiety. This meant she now effectively had two disorders working alongside each other, anorexia and alcohol. She was terrified of being rejected and as a result she felt it was better to spend most of her time on her own and thus (in her mind) avoid the possibility of it occurring. Thus, over time, she became more and more isolated from the other nurses which of course exacerbated the fear.

Her father came to her passing out ceremony as a Nightingale Nurse and she felt at last that in some way she had achieved something that would please him and validate her, even a little, in his mind's eye.

She began a relationship with someone she really liked but it did not last very long and when it ended, she felt as if the world had collapsed in on top of her. In no state to return to work, she went off to a treatment centre in Arizona to help deal with her eating disorder. She was 24 years old.

Towards the end of her treatment, both her parents came over to attend a 'family' week. Her parents were interviewed about their relationship with her and she recalls that instead, her father kept talking to them about his business rather than about his relationship with Becky. Apparently they did eventually break through to him and she describes with some emotion standing on a step at the treatment centre and seeing him with a tear in his eye. It was a moment, she said, that she will never forget as she had never seen him show any emotion ever before.

On her return to London she went back to her nursing work and shortly afterwards met David, her current husband. It was a whirlwind romance and she married him within the year. At last she felt her problems were over and told her father not to worry about her any longer. Unbeknownst to her he had liver cancer and

185

within 2 months of her marriage, he died. She was devastated. The man she had spent her life trying desperately to impress and to get closer to was gone and his death signalled the real beginning of her alcoholism.

She realised she was drinking too much and began to feel the shame and guilt of allowing herself to do so. It didn't stop her. If anything, it encouraged her to drink more. She found she was still driven to succeed in some way in order to assuage her fear of being a 'failure' as his daughter and thus she tried out a number of business ideas which (despite her being very good at them) in the end proved unviable, once again feeding her belief that she was a failure. More pressures developed (often of her own creation) and so the drinking became heavier.

Needing to be doing something to keep herself busy, she went back to nursing with a very pleasant job in the fracture clinic. All was well until she was promoted to a day surgery unit which was a much more stressful environment and included a lot of work in theatre. Her drinking became more severe to ease the stress. The consequences of this slowly became more visible when her hands began shaking uncontrollably when in morning theatre. So embarrassed was she by this that she gave up hospital nursing altogether, promising herself she would find simpler nursing work in a clinic nearby which never happened. She became more isolated, more aloof and of course, drank even more.

Becky's family finally convinced her to check in to the Priory in Chelmsford to 'dry out'. She learnt a lot, but it didn't work as it wasn't her decision. Over the next few years she checked into two more clinics, both of which she checked herself out of and none of which had any real effect. Her drinking persisted, getting worse and worse and with it came more of the shame she felt as a result. Things took a further turn for the worse when she lost her driving licence and became grounded, giving her reason to increase her drinking.

In her lucid moments, she realised the effect it was having on the family, so David and Becky together took the decision to move her into a flat in Woodbridge, close to where the kids were at school so she could see them as and when she needed to. That was the intention; the reality was that this 'freedom' allowed her compulsion to consume her and drive her into complete despair. With no roles to play and no routines to fulfil, she ate little and remained drunk or in 'blackout' most of the time. She looked dreadful and walked around in a stupor, much to the horror of all those who knew her.

Yet paradoxically, it was exactly what she needed to do. One day alone, physically, spiritually and mentally broken, she realised she had reached the end. She couldn't take it anymore. She had reached rock bottom.

But as these thoughts passed through her mind, a glimpse of hope emerged. From deep within, an intuitive feeling welled up that seemed to grasp her by the shoulders and shake her vigorously and she realised then that she did NOT want to die. She wanted to live, to love, to be free from this burden and to become the good mother she so desperately wanted to be. She knew what had to be done and this time it was she who decided to go back to the Priory. This time she really meant it. It was, for Becky, the turning point.

The first week of withdrawal was a living hell, exacerbated of course by her increased consumption. She spent 28 days recovering there with familiar and caring staff making genuine progress and this time, when she left, she made a conscious effort to follow the Twelve Step Recovery Programme1 which all recovering alcoholics are asked to maintain.

The first step, admitting that one cannot control one's addiction is the most crucial. Once this step has been embraced, all other steps follow. Taking full responsibility for what has happened and indeed for one's own recovery is crucial if it is to succeed. In Becky's case, the realisation that God was there meant she felt she wasn't alone, that someone else was there beside her as she took these challenging steps forward into a new way of life.

I take up the interview from there.

Q1. What has shaped your life since then? What are you doing now and how do you feel about yourself? Do you feel quite different to how you felt before?

I had to make it work. Despite my fears, I embraced Alcoholics Anonymous. I got myself a 'sponsor', a previous alcoholic who acts as a mentor, who guided me through the next steps I needed to take. Even today she is always there for me, good days or bad days and that is amazing. AA is not about telling people what to do. It is about learning from others who have succeeded in maintaining their sobriety over a period of time and how they have coped with varying situations. Each meeting is very powerful and deeply moving.

Q2. What is it that creates an addiction? Why do you need an addiction in the first place?

It starts with deep-rooted painful emotions which cannot be expressed in a normal healthy way, typical examples being fear and anger. It is in seeking a way to numb these painful feelings that addictive behaviour begins. Alcohol is of course one way of numbing the pain. For the alcoholic, once the pattern is established, the formula becomes a necessary 'coping' mechanism. It is the equivalent of treating an illness with poison as it becomes a never ending cycle. The more the alcoholic drinks, the more shame and guilt they feel (added to by the denial) and thus requires more alcohol to numb the heightened negative emotions. So what begins as a way to control painful emotions has the end effect of a total loss of control. It gradually manifests into an extremely destructive life-threatening illness affecting their entire life and in particular, their loved ones.

Alcoholics Anonymous is a self-help maintenance programme where the addict can share their feelings and emotions with honesty in a safe environment. We follow the Twelve Steps to Recovery* voluntarily and on a daily basis. By doing so, the addict slowly takes responsibility for their emotions in a constructive and healthy way, create a balanced life and achieve measures of success which were unimaginable while the addict was in the grip of their illness.

Regular meetings are essential to maintaining sobriety and in order to remind us of where we were. The newcomer to the meetings is always the most important person as their own desperation is a reminder to the others that it simply is not worth having that first drink into relapse. Also, by attending regular meetings, we are encouraged to take on responsibilities within the fellowship, all part of building up accountability and trust and rebuilding confidence in ourselves and our fellows.

Of course it is possible for the addict, once drinking has ceased, to 'cross-addict' to something less harmful such as food or exercise. However, following the Twelve Step Recovery Programme1 prevents these 'tangents' affecting our daily lives and a balance can be found. But the AA message is fundamental - alcohol is the 'killer' addiction and TOTAL abstinence for life is required.

Q3. Having inspirational ideas is one thing – putting them into practise with optimism is an entirely different thing altogether and that requires a level of self-confidence and self-trust. Clearly this was lacking in the past, but in the process of going through the fall, you appear to have made contact with your intuitive self. Has this made you feel different about yourself?

I have recognised now how intuitive I am and my creativity has now emerged powerfully in my art. Certainly very central to me has been my spiritual faith, particularly after a discipleship course I took last year. I take one day at a time and handle each challenge as it occurs, rather than letting it fester and become overpowering. One very important point is that I have recognised how debilitating the emotion of resentment is, something many of us feel a lot of the time, not realising how harmful it is for us. I have learnt to recognise it and let it go. I still like my quiet times, but I now love the stimulation of good conversation, being with people and taking an interest in their lives, rather than being so focused on my own.

Winter – by Becky Overy-Owen

Q4. When did you start painting and how else has your life changed?

I started painting on my discipleship course and have been somewhat amazed at my ability to express my feelings and emotions on canvas. I never realised I could paint like this. I love vibrant colours and I find now that some of the scenes, shadows and colours that I come across in the landscape when I am running, I now transfer to the canvas which is very satisfying. The sky is so amazing with its constantly changing shapes and forms.

I also take my Burmese mountain dog (who is now a registered 'pat' dog) on visits to residential homes and the residents absolutely adore her. Bringing a spark of light to the lives of some of these people whose lives are often very drab is very satisfying and I really love doing that.

I am now secretary to the local AA fellowship and I also now have someone I sponsor (someone who is new to the fellowship) which adds to my responsibilities. I also regularly share my story with other fellowships and in my church in the hope that it helps others to relate it to their own struggles and perhaps helps them in their own recovery.

I am also training for next year's London Marathon so that takes up a lot of time and effort as well.

Q5. As you move forward, do you make decisions based more on 'reason and evidence' or are you willing to take the risk of listening to your intuition and follow your inner voice?

This is a constant struggle for me. Because of my impulsive nature and the trouble it has got me into in the past, in my everyday life I find I have to make more measured decisions. Through my prayer I ask for 'God's will, not mine', and I trust that he is right, and time and again it has proved to be so. However from my creative perspective, I use my intuition in a way that I never have before and it is allowing so many new ideas to come forward. I just have to be measured in the way I apply it.

Q6. Most self-help books encourage us to have goals to aim at. This of course gets things done, but there is another strain of thought that suggests that having a blueprint for the entire process seems to negate the possibility of any additional creative intervention. In other words in adopting the process, we sell ourselves short. How do you feel about the concept of 'releasing the expectations of outcome', now that you have come through the hoop?

I find that having too strong a goal creates pressure and pressure is part of the whole problem. It is pressure that encourages addictive behaviour. I do however find that I can take pressure off myself more now by praying through it, knowing that whatever happens is God's will. The world around us is evolving fast, particularly now and so it makes complete sense to be prepared to have a flexible outcome.

Q7. If someone came to you asking for advice on what to do in order to pursue their dreams, given all your experiences to date, what would you say?

They must enjoy what they are doing or intend to do and to be doing it for their own reasons, rather than to satisfy others. They should listen closely to their intuition. They should discuss it with others but choose carefully who they counsel as the wrong people can be very disheartening. Don't rush into anything too impulsively and don't look for instant success and gratification. Another thing: don't give up because things are going wrong or not working out. Everything takes time to develop.

This whole experience, especially after hitting the bottom so hard made me realise I was not who I thought I was – a worthless individual. I always assumed everyone else was right and never gave myself any credit, never realising that I had so much to offer. It has been a very liberating process and I look at each day with gratitude.

Another thing we haven't touched on is ego. I didn't think I had any ego being as I was but I have subsequently realised I had and have a huge ego. It was simply serving me in a negative way, a kind of self-pitying way, blaming everyone else for everything. Today, in recovery, I am very aware of it. One has to be very careful not to allow the ego free reign. There is so much more to us than just the ego.

Conclusion

Becky has been through an exceptionally challenging time. To hit the bottom, to feel so wretched and useless that there is no point in living any longer must be so awful that none of us can quite imagine what it must be like. Yet in that moment, the desire to live, to love and to be loved caused her to begin a process of recovery that is remarkable and on-going to this day.

Until that moment her life had been somewhat dominated by fear; fear of failing as a daughter, fear of rejection, fear of messing up, fear of failing as a mother and much more. What followed was a process of facing her fears, not as if in a battle but walking into them, embracing them, and realising that they were effectively of her own creation. This does not mean that she no longer feels these fears; rather it means that she understands them and their impulsive nature. She knows she can take a few deep breaths, separate herself from the fear and see the bigger picture. She can also pray. The Twelve Step Recovery Programme provides a solid anchor around which she can cast her line and it will remain there until she no longer needs it.

In short, what Becky has discovered is firstly who she really is, secondly what she has to offer and thirdly that she is not alone. She now understands her ego and the power it has over her. She recognises the rules she must live by and has embraced them by choice. She is no longer ashamed of her past and speaks of her experience in a liberated way. She has come to terms with her strengths and weaknesses and her confidence is growing every day.

Clearly there are many people who like Becky have made a remarkable recovery from alcoholism but perhaps what is not always recognised is the extraordinary progress they have made. When society speaks of success, it generally refers to financial, managerial, sports or 'artistic' success. Very rarely is it mentioned in relation to the triumph of the human spirit over really extraordinary odds, such as those experienced through alcoholism. And yet that is what it is and every day is part of that on-going success. One day at a time.

[1] *The Twelve Steps of Alcoholics Anonymous*
http://www.alcoholics-anonymous.org.uk/?pageid=56

The heart of the suggested program of personal recovery is contained in Twelve Steps describing the experience of the earliest members of the Society:

1. We admitted we were powerless over alcohol - that our lives had become unmanageable.
2. Came to believe that a Power greater than ourselves could restore us to sanity.
3. Made a decision to turn our will and our lives over to the care of God as we understood Him.
4. Made a searching and fearless moral inventory of ourselves.
5. Admitted to God, to ourselves and to another human being the exact nature of our wrongs.
6. Were entirely ready to have God remove all these defects of character.
7. Humbly asked Him to remove our shortcomings.
8. Made a list of all persons we had harmed, and became willing to make amends to them all.
9. Made direct amends to such people wherever possible, except when to do so would injure them or others.
10. Continued to take personal inventory and when we were wrong promptly admitted it.
11. Sought through prayer and meditation to improve our conscious contact with God as we understood Him, praying only for knowledge of His will for us and the power to carry that out.
12. Having had a spiritual awakening as the result of these steps, we tried to carry this message to alcoholics and to practice these principles in all our affairs.

19

Conclusion - Where to now?

"It is only with the heart that one can see rightly; what is essential is invisible to the eye."

Antoine De Saint-Exupery

The purpose of this book has been to offer a new way of thinking about ourselves in a rapidly shifting world. There are many changes occurring and how we deal with them and move forward is critically important. It demands a new perception by those who are willing to stand up, think differently and lead the world forward.

The challenge for most of us is that our lives are heavily influenced by the past, be it our own experiences or our wider history. It is as if we are in a tunnel and that tunnel is projected forwards, embracing our present and our future. Most of us are trying to construct our present and future as a continuation of our past, as can be witnessed by our ineffective efforts to solve the current world economic crisis. Unfortunately the tunnel limits our potentials and we simply cannot see the wider opportunities out there. We need to move away from our limited perceptions, step out of the tunnel and expose ourselves to a future of infinite possibilities.

According to Marcia Schafer of 'Beyond Zebra®'[1], there are essentially three main groups of people in the world today who make up the vast population of the planet. In recognising these groups, we see very simply how the world's population divides. This division is not affected by culture, race or religious upbringing. It has to do with the intrinsic makeup of the individuals themselves.

The first of these groups is made up of people who are very

self-empowered; they are not constrained by history, what others might tell them to think, nor do they follow religious or political ideologies. Their power comes from within. They listen very carefully to their intuition and blended together with their creativity and intellect, they are finding new and very powerful ways forward.

The second group of people are those who are starting to look beyond the restrictive tunnel. They are standing at the threshold and looking left and right, up and down and are genuinely interested in finding out more about how to move forward. Most however are still tied to their history, their political and religious affiliations and as a consequence they are feeling their way ahead gingerly. They are willing to consider new ideas and perceptions that in the past they may have rejected but they need to feel 'comfortable' before stepping across the threshold. What they are recognising is that the old ways do not necessarily fit any more and they need new answers to the many questions that arise.

The third group is very entrenched in who they are and what they believe. Their position is that anything that violates their comfort zones is seen as the enemy. They are basically intolerant. They cannot accept other perceptions that might challenge the tenet of their existence as in order to do so, they would need to question their own reality and this is a no-go area. They cannot be questioned. They demand that we see things their way as there is no other way. They are typically made up of religious and political fundamentalists of all different persuasions and when pressed are willing to perform acts of violence (sometimes extreme) in order to maintain their positions. This is not a small group. It is far bigger than we might care to believe and currently holds a great deal of the power in the world today.

Recognising these groups helps us to understand how and why things happen. It also helps us to figure out where we stand and into which group we fit. This in turn helps us to understand our responses to the Eight Critical Questions.

The Eight Critical Questions

All eight of these questions raise important issues which need contemplation over a period of time if they are to be of benefit. Here briefly are key points that each chapter raises.

Whose rules are you following and why? Have you begun to notice certain perceptions you have about who you are and where you fit into society? How about the people around you? Have you noticed how easy it is to follow certain conventions, simply because others do too? How does this affect your stance on 'us' and 'them' attitudes? Has it helped you reconsider your own comfort zone? Can you see how some of these attachments could limit your progress? Have you begun a process of taking ownership of the rules by which you live?

Do you really know who you are? Are you now able to distinguish the difference between the egoical self and the intuitive self? Have you noticed how much the ego (guided by the 'filter') dominates your daily thought patterns and the affect it has on your decision making process? Are you now able to step back and take the 'helicopter' view and connect with your intuitive self? Do you recognise the wisdom of taking a few deep breaths to break the egoical hold and help achieve this? How does the world look from this position? Can you see the effect it has on the way you respond to certain situations and how connecting with it more regularly would be to your benefit?

Do you have the courage to make mistakes openly? Do you recognise how the ego can limit your creativity so drastically by encouraging you to take the safe route? Do you see all aspects of life as an adventure? Have you noted the wisdom gained from standing on one leg and feeling the 'wobble', the body over-correcting? Do you recognise that the intuitive self is non-judgemental and allows us to see the wisdom of our errors and of course also the funny side?

Are you willing to embrace change? Have you recognised the external anchors in your life? Have you noticed how your willingness to remain tied to them so rigidly limits your ability to embrace change? Have you yet recognised that there is nothing you have to do in order to find your own internal anchor other than to relax into the splendour of your Intuitive self? Considering the extraordinary achievements of Nelson Mandela, have you realised quite how empowering this internal anchor is?

Do you honestly trust yourself? Are you still at the mercy of your egoical self and your filter, where comparing yourself to others is a key perspective? Are you able to see that your uniqueness is itself the golden chalice and that you are delightfully different? Do you have the courage to step out of line and trust that things will work out? Do you recognise that we create our own realities? Do you see that if we live from a position of misery and pain, that is what we attract and if we live from a position of joy then that is what we experience? Are you willing to rethink the whole concept of setting goals and release the expectations of outcome?

What is the tone of your communication with others? Are you genuine and honest about yourself and in your dealings or do you have two sets of values? Do you recognise the need in others for validation and that from their perspective, they are right? Are you a good listener and are you generous in your dealings with others? Do you look for mutual interests in finding agreement? Have you recognised the important role your intuitive self plays in your communication?

Are you a true or a selfish leader? How do you see your own leadership style? Are you aware of the huge responsibility you carry and how it affects the lives of those you lead intimately? Have you noted the benefits of servant leadership? Do you recognise that by empowering those you lead, they will return the favour? Do you recognise the critical role the intuitive self plays in being a great leader?

What is your passion? What are your dreams? What is it that inspires you, that flicks a switch on when you think about it? Are you free enough to let it blossom? Like Ghandi and Betty Makoni, does that passion come welling up from deep inside? If it isn't forthcoming, would it be helpful to free yourself up more from your limitations to allow it the freedom to emerge? Can you see the power of determination, of keeping going, knowing that it will work out in the end?

By freeing yourself from your built-in constraints and the limitations of the filter (the fear of failure) and allowing yourselves not just to create the idea but to pursue it with passion, you will set a ball rolling, creating opportunities that were unthinkable a few weeks or months before. Your determination itself will create the path forward. Trust yourself and your abilities and keep focused on what it is you are trying to achieve and you will be assisted along your path in ways you could never have imagined.

The Mold Breakers

By reading about and feeling into the lives of those who have broken the mold, you will have gained some insight into how others have harnessed this extraordinary power in their own way. They help to clarify that this is real and not some whimsical idea.

Steve Jobs provides what appears to be an extraordinarily simple approach to life in the short paragraph in chapter 13 but do not be fooled. To genuinely live life in the way he suggests requires, for most of us, a serious conscious adjustment. It requires contemplating where we are now and what we need to do in order to follow his guidelines. Bear in mind that whilst one can shift from one approach to another instantly by choice, in order for it to become sustainable, it needs us to relax into it and own it. It needs to become part of us, rather than a 'technique' we use. That way it becomes a natural part of our everyday lives.

Each of the four interviewees offers a very different perspective on how they live life. Scott Russell is probably the easiest to relate to as his life is the most conventional. Scott keeps his vision simple. He is clear on what he wishes to achieve and has no fear of trying out new ideas. He listens carefully to his intuition and is prepared to take a fair level of risk in order to test out new theories. No goal is set in stone so his business and his progress are constantly changeable at any time. As a result of his shrewd business mind, his determination and a very strong work ethic, he is now a multi-millionaire.

Francois Le Roux offers an entirely different perspective on the whole purpose of life. Unlike Scott, he is not interested in money as an end. He is totally content with a simple and uncomplicated way of life. He rejects the search for perfection and with it the trappings of fame. Whilst conducting his shows or workshops, he does not seek to inspire or change anyone. Rather he feels into the atmosphere of the room, the attendant group and into each participant. No single workshop is the same. Everything is unscripted and as he himself describes, *"therein lies the deeper art, a dialogue of sensitivities, a play with colour, an openness to be human with each other"*. He taps into the intuition and creativity of those around him and offers them, with his encouragement, the opportunity to freely express themselves with raw energy.

Joanna Jones believes that when we are in tune with our passion (whatever it is that truly inspires us), we become filled with energy and a drive that propels us forward, irrespective of the many mistakes we might make along the way or even the doubt that creeps in from time to time. Like Francois, she has no expectation of outcome and as such allows her paintings to evolve in their own way. She also touches on the issue of fear and how easy it is to fall prey to the need to adjust something in order to meet the needs of external demands or pressures. Whilst she spends a lot of time viewing the results of her painting at each stage, her eyes are irrelevant in the act of painting. *"I paint through touch and not through sight. It is not my hands that I use but my whole body – which means I cannot see. I can only feel what I am doing for the duration of the act. Each time I enter a work I privilege my tactile sense over my visual sense."* She describes the way she moves across the canvas as intuitive, allowing her senses, rather than her conscious mind to lead the way.

Becky Overy-Owen shows us how one can be so trapped in fear that the only way out of it is to crash and burn. Yet in the process of crashing, when she felt that the worst possible had happened and she could sink no further, she was gripped by a powerful urge to live and love and began a remarkable process of recovery. Since that time she has moved ahead with a determination and a desire to be her true self. She is no longer running scared of her past, though even without the fear, the temptation for a 'quick drink' is always there. Slowly but surely she is exposing herself more regularly to her natural senses (particularly through her art) and as she feels more sure of herself, so there is a greater willingness to open up to her intuitive self. Whilst still clinging to the side of the tunnel she is looking out, tentatively moving forward into a future of infinite potentials.

Each of these people exhibits what I believe to be vital ingredients to a successful, invigorating and meaningful life. We each come from a different standpoint and what we take from each will be entirely individual and personal.

What stands out in particular in the cases of Steve Jobs, Scott Russell, Francois Le Roux and Joanna Jones is their freedom and courage to be original. They have freed themselves from conventional beliefs and restrictions and had the passion to move ahead in their own particular ways. What Becky Overy-Owen shows us is that it does not matter where we have been or how desperate and despondent we may become, we can always recover and step out of the tunnel – no matter quite how challenging the journey and the prospect might seem.

What I sincerely believe is that if you recognise the power and wisdom of your intuitive self you will begin to relax into who you really are and become less dependent upon external needs, perceptions and the need for verification. By revisiting all eight of the Critical Questions, you will find a way of stepping out across the threshold of the tunnel with greater confidence and move forward into a life of genuine purpose, meaning and originality. There will no longer be a need to have two sets of values, one for work and one for Sunday best. Your life will not be one of simply DOING. It will be much more about BEING and Richard Branson's perception of the future will resonate. As Branson said, *"Never has there been a more exciting time for all of us to explore this great next frontier where the boundaries between work and purpose are merging into one, where doing good, really is good for business."* [2]

Through effective leadership and genuine encouragement, more people will become inspired to do the same. You will become the match bearers, those who light up the way for others as they move forward on their own individual and inspiring journeys.

I wish you well.

[1] *These three groups were determined by Marcia Schafer, MBA of 'Beyond Zebra®' (www.beyondzebra.com) through her own detailed research and are used regularly by her as a descriptive tool in her work.*

[2] *From the introduction to 'Screw Business as Usual' by Richard Branson, Ebury 2011.*

Visit **www.cultivating-intuition.com** *for more background, links to talks, images, references and a regular blog of new ideas.*

An afterthought

Acting on an intuitive impulse

Orlando Barley outside the Lloyds of London building with his sign

Orlando Barley graduated from Durham University, UK in June 2011. So put off was he by the stories of assessment days, interviews and internships (work without income) that so many people had to go through before being finally offered a paid job that he simply never followed the conventional route of submitting an application. It almost seemed loaded against the applicant as there were so many others out there with equally high qualifications.

With the prospect of unemployment looming, Orlando decided he needed to be noticed. He was more than just an application form, but how could he attract interest? How could he make himself stand out? He discussed this with his friends. They flipped a number of intuitive ideas around and one of those was to stand outside the Lloyds of London building in the city with a sign saying he was looking for a job in Insurance.

The idea was a good one but who in their right mind would stand outside the Lloyds building waving a sign? Who would have the gall to do that? After all, it broke all conventions and the chances were people would shun him as they might a beggar. On the other hand, maybe some would take notice and if they didn't, the chances were they wouldn't remember him the next day anyway.

Orlando decided the risk to his ego and his reputation were worth taking and on the morning of 22nd September, he took several deep breaths and presented himself, in a suit, at the door of the Lloyds of London building, with a sign announcing his search. He stood there the whole day and approached no-one. Rather, his sign did the talking for him. It filtered out those who didn't care (or who had no interest) as they simply walked by but many stopped, intrigued, and by the end of the day he had 22 business cards in his pocket.

Following up on those leads, he was given four interviews and received three job offers. Today Orlando works in the Lloyds building, employed by one of those people who stopped to talk to him that day. He achieved something that would have been far harder to achieve had he used conventional means. He harnessed an intuitive idea and had the courage to step out of his comfort zone, willing to look a fool if it didn't work out.

As he said later, 'taking this very direct approach saved a lot of time'. He now reaps the benefits.

About the author

The Marketing Blurb

James Maberly is an author, an artist and a social entrepreneur. Born in Kenya and brought up in Zimbabwe, he lived an idyllic early life on a farm, which pretty much meant boarding school as soon as he was old enough. There followed three years in the British Army with the Royal Scots Dragoon Guards, then art studies at the Norwich School of Art, specialising in sculpture and drawing, attaining a BA (Hons) in Fine Art. This led to four happy years as an art lecturer at Suffolk College. He continues to produce drawings and sculpture and also now teaches Intuitive Drawing from his studio.

James has never lost interest in Africa and Zimbabwe in

particular. He founded a charity to care for farmers and farm-workers whose lives were devastated by the farm invasions, which led to an interest in the processes of negotiation and mediation. Further studies in this area have enabled him to begin the first attempts at bringing the various stakeholders together.

He is also an accomplished public speaker having lectured on self-reliance in the past and has spoken to various think tanks about the challenges currently being faced in Zimbabwe.

The Real Person

James is also clumsy, hardly ever on time, pretty much deaf in one ear (to the extreme irritation of his family), untidy and wears a tie so little now that he gets a rash on his neck each time he wears one. He adores his family, treasures his friends, regularly wears a kikoy and loves bananas.

He is married with four children and lives in Suffolk in the UK.

Visit **www.cultivating-intuition.com** *for more background, links to talks, images, references and a regular blog of new ideas.*

Permissions

The author gratefully acknowledges permission from the following additional sources to reprint material in their control:

a) Anthony J. D'Angelo, Author of The College Blue Book and Rich Grad Poor Grad.
b) Peter L. Salk, M.D. President, Jonas Salk Legacy Foundation, 7459 High Avenue, La Jolla, CA 92037
c) Pamela Kribbe, from www.jeshua.net.
d) Penguin books, 80 Strand, London WC2R 0RL www.penguin.co.uk
e) Hay House, Inc., P.O. Box 5100, Carlsbad, CA 92018-5100
f) Mrs Kathy Eldon, The Dan Eldon Foundation. www.daneldon.org
g) BBC Commercial Agency, BBC Vision, Room 4600 | BBC White City London W12 7TS | T. 0208 752 4130 | M. 07525 403953 www.bbc.co.uk
h) Permissions Assistant, SAGE Publications Ltd, 1 Oliver's Yard, 55 City Road, London, EC1Y 1SP , UK
i) Carol Craig, Chief Executive, Centre for Confidence and Well-being www.centreforconfidence.co.uk.
j) Permissions Coordinator, Beacon Press, 25 Beacon Street, Boston, MA 02108.
k) Charles Handy, Suffolk, UK.
l) The Random House Group Limited, Archive and Library, 1 Cole Street Crown Park, Rushden, Northants, NN10 6RZ
m) Tony King, Jillifar Amor, Christina Orrock, Lou and Xenia Dautzenberg all of Suffolk, UK.
n) BC strip reprinted with permission of John L. Hart FLP. www.johnhartstudios.com .

32329432R00123

Made in the USA
Charleston, SC
15 August 2014